The Missing

The Story Of An Undefeated Life

By Doreen Ashley

Contributions from the sale of this book will be made to support the work of OPEN DOORS UK

For Arthur

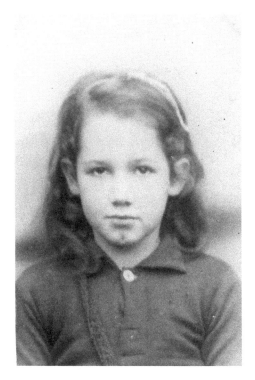

Based on a true story

Perhaps it is a good thing that we don't know what our future holds; if we did, we might not have the courage to walk that way.

THE END OF OUR STREET

We all played together at the end of our street.
Most of the kids were scruffy and thin
At the end of the war, with rationing in.
It meant nothing to us – the news of the dead,
Or how our parents had kept us all fed.
We just played together at the end of our street.

We grew up together at the end of our street.
Some went to high school, with uniforms and books,
The rest stayed behind and went to St Luke's.
By the light of the street lamps we started our wishing
For boyfriends and girlfriends and romance and kissing!
Our lives began changing at the end of our street.

We drifted apart at the end of our street.
We all had new interests that took us away,
Too busy and grown up to come out to play.
No longer bothered about larking and sporting,
We're all dressed up smart and going out courting!
No playing out now at the end of our street.

No longer together at the end of our street
We all journeyed off to find distant lands,
With youthful ambition and full of our plans.
The children we were gone forever away,
Now we are grown up with no time to play!
Goodbye, all my playmates at the end of our street

BACK IN TIME

Sylvia alighted from the coach and stood bathed in the morning sunshine, gazing in wonder at the scene before her. This is where it had all begun – her dream and her downfall!

She felt strange standing in what looked like a foreign country but was, in fact, Salford – the place of her childhood. But there was not one thing that she recognised here. She wandered around trying to catch a glimpse of something familiar but there was nothing. In her mind she could see the docks and the factories overshadowing the rows of old terraced houses in Sunnyside Street, a place where the sun hardly ever shone. Today she was surrounded by the magnificent buildings of the Salford Quays, the Lowry Centre, the University and the BBC Headquarters.

With a shrug, having satisfied her curiosity, she thought she could walk away and forget the past but she was wrong. She was overwhelmed by the memories of who she used to be. In her imagination, she could hear the voices of the children playing in the street and the voice of the person she was, calling out to be heard. As a child, she had cherished a dream; as an adult, that dream had turned into a nightmare. Now, in the safety of the present, she allowed herself to look back.

It all began in the streets around the Manchester Ship Canal – but it didn't end there!

DOWN AT THE DOCKS

'Run, Albert! Run!' Frantically he repeated the words to himself as he ran out of the dock gates. Even though he had been expecting the summons, his heart had skipped a beat when the foreman had shouted to him across the canal in his strong Lancashire accent, 'Albert, cum on, lad. Yer needed at 'ome, no time to waste.'

His mates called out 'Good luck!' as he raced past them and caught the tram just as it was about to leave. He took a seat, shivering from the cold winter air, his mind racing as the tram swayed slowly and monotonously on its journey, oblivious to his turbulent thoughts and pounding heart.

He jumped from the tram as his stop approached, his stomach churning and nausea threatening to overwhelm him. 'Please God, don't let it happen again,' he cried, as he ran down the street.

Reaching his house, he crashed through the front door, bumping into their next-door neighbour, Mrs Begley, who was waiting calmly for him to arrive home. 'It's alright, son,' she reassured him. 'Don't panic. The midwife is in with her.'

In his haste, Albert forgot his manners and pushed past the kindly lady, ignoring her reassurance. 'Mary! Mary! Are yea all right?' he called, running up the lobby towards the parlour.

He didn't make it through the parlour door, let alone reach his wife. He was obstructed by the formidable form of the midwife. This was her domain; the front room was now a delivery suite where she had indisputable authority and no man was allowed.

He retreated reluctantly; despite her intimidating manner, he knew that his wife was in good hands. He only wished he could see her just for a moment and promise her that it wouldn't be like the last time when their newborn baby had died. But he knew he couldn't; a t this stage, not even the capable and indomitable Nurse Spencer could guarantee that.

As he retraced his steps, he took his youngest son, Arthur, from Mrs Begley's arms. Calming the child's tears, he thanked their kind and capable neighbour who had already taken the older boys to school. Now all he could do was wait.

The only people in the room during the labour on that significant day when Sylvia was born were the midwife and Mrs Begley. Albert, according to the custom during a home birth, was relegated to the kitchen. He gave Arthur his breakfast of bread and jam and anxiously paced the floor as he listened to the midwife's voice from behind the closed parlour door.

From his experience of previous births, he kept the kettle of boiling water ready and set about preparing the gruel – that was his job! Providing the new mother with a bowl of gruel after the birth was the standard practice after a home delivery. It was supposed to assist her in establishing breastfeeding and commonly believed to help recovery, enabling her to get back on her feet as soon as possible. However, it was not the gruel that motivated Mary; like many women in those days, she had other children demanding her attention. Lying in bed was not an option!

Eventually the midwife flung open the parlour door and announced, 'It's a girl. Come and meet your daughter, Mr Frangleton.'

Albert rushed in, relieved to know all was well and that, after the birth of four boys and a stillbirth, this baby was a girl! Above all, he was thankful that it had been a safe delivery. As they knew all too well, although home deliveries were the norm, there was always the risk of complications that often resulted in the loss of the baby.

The likelihood of a stillbirth or neonatal death was a fact of life in the 1930s and 40s. Without doubt, that thought had been in the back of their minds throughout the nine months' pregnancy; they remembered how devastated they had been the last time when their baby boy had been stillborn. But for now they were happy that a new life had entered the world, even if their happiness would be short lived, for their euphoria following the birth was inevitably tempered by the challenge of another mouth to feed. It was a familiar situation for those living by the docks and in the shadow of the factories and mills of Salford.

But today was a day of rejoicing. Baby Sylvia had arrived.

THE WAR – THE BABY AND THE FUNERAL

Sylvia grew up by the docks along the Manchester Ship Canal, where her impoverished lifestyle held no promise of a bright future. For her parents, Mary and Albert, the future looked bleak and providing for their growing family became more challenging with each new birth. Added to their anxiety was the threat of war with Germany.

In September 1939 the threat became a reality and the declaration of war with Germany was broadcast to the nation by the prime minister, Neville Chamberlain. Initially Albert was spared from conscription into the army for, as a docker working on the Manchester Ship Canal, his job was classified as a reserved occupation. However, at the height of the war in 1941 the Government was forced to recruit younger men from the reserved occupations and Albert was enlisted to join the troops in France.

At the time, Mary was expecting her sixth child. The three older boys had been evacuated to a farm in Garstang in the north of England. Despite the imminent arrival of their baby, Albert had to leave Mary and the two children, Sylvia and Bernard, age four and two years old, to depend on the support of his father and sister, Ada.

After only a few weeks away, Albert received a telegram informing him that Mary had given birth to a son. He was granted compassionate leave and arrived home to find that the birth had not gone well. Sadly, the baby died two days later.

For Sylvia, this event was her earliest memory of a death in the family. Her parents had given no explanation to her or her brothers about the birth of a baby or how or why it had died. Although the children were anxious and naturally inquisitive, they were not encouraged to ask questions. It was not customary to talk to children about such things.

Consequently, the arrival of an undertakers' hearse a few days later aroused their curiosity. Sylvia was playing in the street with some little girls, and the boys were kicking a ball around in the middle of the road, when the hearse drew up outside their house. At the sight of the big, black, shiny vehicle the children stopped their play and crowded round to see a small coffin being removed from the car and carried solemnly into the house by two men dressed in black. The neighbours along the street came out to stand on their doorsteps to watch in respectful silence.

Sylvia stood with the other children as they gazed wide-eyed at the strange scene before them. Her father appeared at the front door with her mother beside him, crying. The coffin was carried inside and the door closed behind them. When the men in black reappeared a little time later, the neighbours retreated behind their own front doors shaking their heads sadly as the hearse moved slowly away. The children returned to their play.

Before the funeral, the baby's tiny coffin was kept in the darkened parlour with the curtains closed. The neighbours in the street drew their own parlour curtains in sympathy with the bereaved family and called at the house to pay their respects and whisper their condolences. As was the custom, one of them made a door-to-door collection in the immediate vicinity to help cover the cost of the funeral.

On the day of the funeral, Sylvia remembered one of her relatives taking her into the parlour and lifting her up to see the baby lying in quiet solitude. They stood close to the coffin so that she could see him – a beautiful porcelain doll in a white gown with the fragrance of lilies filling the room. She was told his name was Graham and that he was her brother. She remembered feeling curious but not in any way sad like the adults.

Inevitably Albert had to return to his regiment, leaving Mary and his sister and father to cope with the aftermath of their emotional ordeal. With the war on and Albert away in the army, Mary, still grieving the loss of her baby, resumed her responsibility for the children's safety during the air raids.

Living close to the docks and the Manchester Ship Canal, the homes in their neighbourhood were easy targets. Mary spent many nights during the blackout sitting by gas light beside the dying embers of the coal fire at home, waiting for the dreaded sirens warning of an imminent air raid. It was arranged that, at the sound of the siren, Mary would take two-year-old Bernard to a shelter at the end of the street; her sister-in-law Ada and Granddad would arrive to take Sylvia, who was awake and screaming at the sound of the siren, to another shelter.

Bewildered and frightened, Sylvia would sit on her Granddad's knee as they huddled together alongside their neighbours in the dim, cold light of the air-raid shelter, becoming increasingly alarmed each time the terrifying sound of a bomb exploded in the streets around them.

At daylight, after a sleepless night, the weary and apprehensive adults would emerge from the shelter at the sound of the all-clear siren to survey the damage before heading off to work.

On some nights Ada served as a volunteer warden in the Air Raid Patrol, where local men and women worked alongside the fire brigade putting out the fires started by the incendiary bombs. They worked tirelessly throughout the night and often, along with everyone else, they left directly for work the following morning.

THE DOLL

One day, when Sylvia's father was home on leave, a very special visitor arrived. Sylvia clearly remembered the first time she met him. She was waiting with her parents and Auntie Ada and Granddad in the street outside their house. The early morning rain had stopped and the sun was dazzling on the wet cobblestones, reflecting on the shining windows.

She saw him as he turned the corner at the end of the street, long before he reached them as they stood ready to welcome him. Although they were all equally excited, the adults stood warily, hardly allowing themselves to show any emotion. The austere, Lancashire, time-honoured tradition of giving nothing away was etched on their faces, as if showing pleasure was an indulgence to be rationed. Only Ada showed her eagerness and delight. Granddad stood stiffly to one side of the door, reserving his judgement.

Sylvia sensed that this was an important occasion – her parents and Granddad were about to meet her Auntie Ada's 'young man', an American soldier based at a nearby barracks, for the first time. He strode down the street with a relaxed gait and, as he approached, Sylvia could not help jumping up and down in her excitement. As the handsome American reached them, he smiled broadly, completely relaxed and at ease. He gave Ada a hug and then shook hands with everyone else, including Sylvia as she shyly hid behind her mother's skirt!

The brief introductions over, they all turned to follow Ada into the house where she had prepared tea. Just at that moment, the young man reached into his tunic and produced a doll. He crouched down in front of Sylvia and said in his unfamiliar American drawl, 'This is for you, little girl.' His lovely brown eyes smiled at her warmly.

It was a nurse doll with a blue dress and a crisp white apron and nurse's cap. A bright red cross covered the front of her bib. She was the most beautiful thing Sylvia had ever seen, with a pretty face and lovely golden curls. In that magical moment, Sylvia gazed enthralled at the handsome American, clasping the doll close to her heart.

Not long afterwards, before moving on to his next mission, the handsome American and Ada became engaged to be married. Sylvia never saw him again.

The doll became Sylvia's most treasured possession and constant companion. She invested in her all the love and affection she was unable to express in the emotionally-deprived environment at home. It was the doll that inspired Sylvia to become a nurse. Of course, back then she did not know the demands and challenges that would confront her in the years to come before she achieved her goal. But, despite her fragile and uncertain world and the indifferent and cheerless future ahead of her, the thought and the dream grew unwaveringly into a firm resolve with the simple innocent faith of a child.

Sylvia nurtured that cherished dream throughout her childhood, believing that it would become reality one day. She was totally unaware of the profound words spoken by Jesus in the Bible: 'As a man thinks in his heart, so is he', and: 'Out of the abundance of the heart, the mouth speaks'.

Sylvia did not know then that the thoughts of the heart are revealed by the words that we speak, and that our thoughts and words influence the direction of our lives. But instinctively, even as a child, she thought and spoke her heart's desire that one day she would, without a doubt, become a nurse despite the lack of any encouragement and many setbacks.

ENID BLYTON AND *SUNNY STORIES*

Sylvia's Auntie Ada and Granddad played an important role in her upbringing. She especially remembered their home because she spent so much time there as a child. Although there was no love lost between her mother and Auntie Ada, it was Ada who made life more bearable for them all by her unstinting help with the upbringing of the children. Sylvia, in particular, received more of her aunt's attention than her brothers because, being a girl, she was apparently easier to handle than the boys.

Ada had a great influence over her; it was with gratitude Sylvia recalled that, as a child, she caught a glimpse of what a normal home life could be. Looking after her whenever she could was Ada's contribution to the rearing of her brother's growing brood. Besides working full time in the printing trade in Manchester, she made dresses for Sylvia on her old Singer sewing machine with second-hand dress material. For the boys, she knitted jumpers, scarves, balaclavas and mittens.

In Sylvia's early years, Ada represented the maternal love her mother was incapable of providing. The atmosphere in her aunt's home was a haven of peace and tranquillity, giving her the opportunity to grow and develop in ways that were impossible in the overcrowded environment in her own home, with the children playing and squabbling in one room often developing into open hostility and fighting. Unhappily, their home was a place where there were few signs of affection even towards the babies and young children. Sylvia could not remember ever being hugged or kissed by anyone, not even her Auntie Ada.

It was Auntie Ada who encouraged her to paint and draw, allowing her to spend hours painting china plates and various other pieces of crockery with her little tin of paints. Ada taught her to read and bought her *Sunny Stories* comics and Enid Blyton books; she always responded to the child's cries of,

'Read to me, Auntie, read to me,' long before Sylvia was able to read them for herself.

Sometimes Ada would take Sylvia by bus into Manchester on Saturdays, where they spent the afternoon window shopping in the city centre. Ada bought freshly ground coffee at the well-known Kardoma coffee shop, where coffee beans were sold (not to be confused with the coffee shops we know today, where customers are served coffee). Sylvia was fascinated as she watched the coffee beans being weighed and ground at the counter in front of them then packed into little brown-paper parcels. Before returning home, their special treat was to walk through the lovely Piccadilly Gardens to Woolworths, where they sat on high stools at the counter in the café for tea and delicious parkin cake.

There were no such treats in Sylvia's home but despite this, because of Ada's contribution to her upbringing, she enjoyed far more privileges than her brothers. They were not always welcome in Ada's neat and tidy home, where the table was always set with a white tablecloth and china crockery and mealtimes were more organised than the rough-and-ready arrangement in their own home.

Although mealtimes at home did not compare with those at Auntie Ada's, the family did sit down together around the table in their small living room, where nothing matched and where there was no tablecloth. Sylvia, along with the other little ones, sat huddled along the back wall on a wooden bench that their father had 'acquired' from the disused air-raid shelter at the end of the street.

Teatime was the main meal of the day and, from what Sylvia could recall, they were a remarkably well-behaved lot, waiting expectantly to be served. Her mother would dish up the meal with the words, 'If you want any more, you'll have to fill up on bread and jam.' The concept of a second course did not exist in their house.

A BATTLE WITH BUGS

When the war ended circumstances for the Frangleton family, and for many others in their neighbourhood, failed to live up to their expectations. Once victory was declared and the street parties were over, it was assumed that the returning soldiers would be welcomed back as victorious heroes with a bright future ahead them, but their hopes for a more prosperous lifestyle gave way to disillusion and, in many cases, a life of poverty. The threat of the workhouse continued to haunt the poor, even though workhouses had been officially closed since 1930, long before the war.

Following his discharge from the army, Albert secured a job back on the docks and began working again on the Manchester Ship Canal. About the same time, the family were rehoused as part of the government resettlement initiative. This meant moving away from Ada and Granddad to a house across town.

Sylvia remembered that her parents were pleased to be among those selected for rehousing, which was a huge problem for the government at the end of the war. Hundreds of homes in the area had been destroyed during the Blitz and many families still lived in temporary, substandard accommodation close to the bomb sites and surrounded by rubble, so anything that was offered was gladly accepted. However, life in the allocated property turned out to be one of the most harrowing and abhorrent experiences of their lives.

They hadn't been living in their new home for long before their euphoria evaporated. They discovered that the house, being an old dwelling, was infested with bedbugs. These blood-sucking creatures lived in the cracks in the plaster on the walls and in the old wallpaper in the bedrooms. Detecting the warmth of human bodies, they made their way into the family's beds as they lay huddled together asleep. The bugs gorged on their warm bodies throughout the night until they dropped off, bloated with blood. The family awoke each day to discover bites all over them. Sylvia remembered seeing blood-red bugs scurrying away to hide in the cracks of the wooden bedstead as she rose in the morning, scratching.

They were easy prey and, with no baths or hot water, trying to eradicate the bugs was futile; for a long time, the family fought a losing battle. Finally they were forced to vacate the premises while the Council fumigated the entire house, including the furniture and all their clothes.

In the meantime, the whole family had to be bathed and treated with an insecticide at the public wash baths. For the most part, the younger brothers and Sylvia were shielded from the humiliation and embarrassment experienced by the adults. It was undoubtedly more embarrassing for her acutely self-conscious pre-teen brothers.

For Sylvia, the one outstanding impression from that experience was the distinct and obnoxious odour of bedbugs that permeated the place to such an extent that they could be detected simply by walking into a room.

NO PLACE LIKE HOME

Moving across town, the family no longer had the close support of Ada and Granddad; the children especially missed them. Granddad was the one who regularly cut the boys' hair and mended their clogs on his shoe last (they rarely had shoes).

As a young child, Sylvia had always depended on her Auntie Ada. Now, even as a seven year old, the child was proving to be more useful to her mother at home. Without her auntie close by to watch over her, she missed her and became increasingly lonely.

Living closer to the docks, there was more open space for the children to play but, whenever she had the opportunity, Sylvia found refuge in the home of one of her new friends. Although just as poor as her own family, this girl had loving parents and a place that was a safe and happy haven. Sylvia would often spend time with them just to share in the warmth and security of their home. Her best friend's parents welcomed her to join their lively brood whenever she turned up. This was such a stark contrast to the unhappy atmosphere at home, where Sylvia and her brothers hardly ever spent time together as a family with their own parents and where laughter was rare and kind words were few and far apart.

As a young girl, Sylvia spent most of her free time out on the streets or by the docks with her younger brothers. The older boys had paper rounds or hung about in their own gangs. The younger children, out at play, took for granted the sight of huge ships navigating the locks along the Manchester Ship Canal close by.

The significance of seafaring vessels passing through the Mode Wheel lock at the end of the street was lost on them but the lock gates gave them access to a wonderful playground on the occasions they managed to sneak past the policeman on duty at the dock gate. They spent many hours on the bomb sites and in the disused air raid shelters, oblivious to the ugliness surrounding them. Bricks and rubble became their building blocks long before Lego was invented, and health and safety regulations had not even been thought of!

It was sad that the children were happiest anywhere but at home, for Sylvia and her young brothers only knew a kind of happiness when they were out playing together in the street or running free in the fields.

As they grew up, Sylvia and her brothers began to understand just how poor they were compared to some of their friends. In their house every penny counted. The older boys left school at the age of fourteen and started working at one of the local factories. Each of the children, even the younger ones, had jobs before or after school as a matter of necessity to supplement the family income – and not only the boys! Sylvia regularly ran errands before school for an elderly neighbour, and frequently after school too.

The average working man in many of the poorer parts of Lancashire in the early 1940s and into the 1950s was under the fist of his employer, who had the power to hire and fire his employees on a whim. Workers were powerless to oppose or confront their employers in any way for fear of losing their job. The mills and factories were owned by wealthy businessmen. They were referred to by the workers as 'The Masters'; indeed, that is how they were viewed, such was the prevailing subservient mentality among the working classes. That sense of inferiority was passed on to the children, an attitude that Sylvia found hard to throw off well into her teenage and adult years.

By today's standards, Sylvia's world was incredibly simple. For example, children were not expected to notice their mother's advancing pregnancy; when a baby appeared 'out of the blue', they were told it had been brought by the midwife in her nurse's bag! But it was like the stories about Santa Claus:

sooner or later the truth would dawn on them whatever the adults said!

Mothers were expected to remain in bed following a home delivery, with the midwife visiting twice a day during the ten days' lying-in period. But with Albert back at work within a few hours of the birth, and the rest of the family to look after, lying-in was out of the question for Mary.

The high birth rate was the cause of much hardship and family planning was unreliable. It would be several years before Enoch Powell, the Minister of Health, made the contraceptive pill freely available to all women in the UK. When it came in 1961, it was too late for Mary.

_____

PLAYING WITH FIRE

During the school summer holidays, when they were out playing in the fields or by the canal, Sylvia's young brothers often ended up in trouble. They had many escapades trying to outsmart the policeman on duty at the dock gates. It was more fun playing inside the gates, not to mention running in and out of the huge stacks of cargo by the railway that ran alongside the canal. Best of all was the thrill of evading discovery!

One day Sylvia tracked the boys down even though, as usual, they were trying to conceal their whereabouts from her. Excluding her from their plans was quite normal; being a girl, she was considered to be a bit of a nuisance. Once she found them, however, they would reluctantly condescend to let her tag along with them.

One of the reasons they tolerated her was because she could be quite useful. On that particular day they had planned to make a fire in the field; it so happened that she was just the one they needed to run back home and fetch some firewood from their back yard. They assured her that no one would suspect her, a girl, of pinching the wood, and she believed them. Happy to oblige, she ran back home through the back gate and gathered as much wood as she could carry without being seen.

By the time she returned, they had collected a pile of old newspapers, twigs and branches ready to start the fire. The excited group of young boys gathered around Sylvia's brother, Bernard, who had acquired some matches. They were imitating some older boys in the next street who had set fire to a large part of the grassy field the week before. The older boys hadn't let the younger kids anywhere near their spectacular blaze, thereby provoking them into wanting to build a fire of their own. With their ignorance and bravado, the children gave no thought to the danger; they were excited and high on adrenalin. 'It's only going to be a little fire,' they reasoned.

It wasn't only the fire that posed a risk; they would undoubtedly be seen by the policeman patrolling the dock gate. But the idea had run away with them and Sylvia was equally enthralled. It didn't matter that the dock gates were within sight – the boys had chosen this spot because they supposed the fire would be hidden by the hill that lay between them and the policeman's patrol route. They were beyond discovery – or so they thought! Little did the boys know that their fire would provide more excitement than they had bargained for and that Sylvia was to be the cause!

In the post-war days, girls almost always wore dresses; jeans or any kind of trousers were considered unsuitable for them. On the day in question, Sylvia was dressed in one of Auntie Ada's best efforts, a cotton dress made from second-hand dress material. It was a sort of 'princess' dress, white, with a gathered waist, full skirt, sash, and a big bow at the back. It was entirely inappropriate but, since 'make do and mend' was the general rule, a dress made from what was obviously once someone's expensive garment was not uncommon. This one was one of Auntie Ada's more imaginative designs.

The group gathered around Bernard as he produced the matches. There was a moment's silence as, with bated breath, they watched him strike a match and light the fire. This was followed by several anxious minutes as they eagerly crowded round before the flames became visible through the spiralling smoke. Soon, to everyone's delight, the flames shot up. The fire was well and truly ablaze!

They inched forward, moving as close as they could, throwing more sticks into the dancing flames and revelling in their success, unaware of any impending danger.

There was no way of knowing what they had anticipated from that reckless deed but what followed was far beyond their expectations. They stood around enjoying the fire but it was not long before one of the boys spotted the policeman in the distance, strolling towards them.

By this time the flames had really caught on and the acrid smoke was shooting upwards, exposing their position. Panicking, one of the boys shouted, 'It's the copper, stand around with your back to the fire!'

Everyone crowded round at his command, trying to shield the fire from view, hoping it wouldn't be seen by the patrolling officer. Following the boys' example, Sylvia shuffled backwards towards the fire too. Suddenly the now-ferocious flames caught her skirt and she was engulfed in a terrifying blaze.

Instantly Bernard lunged forward and pushed her to the ground. As she landed on the soft earth, screaming frantically, he rolled her in the long grass while the other boys stood by frozen in horror. Then, quick as lightning, as one the boys turned and ran, scattering in all directions.

Bernard struggled as he dragged Sylvia to her feet and beat out the flames at the back of her skirt. He pulled her up and yelled, 'Run!', then set off, racing towards home. Sylvia followed him, running as fast as she could with her smoking dress billowing behind her.

The fire was discovered but the children were not! They managed to disappear before the policeman could catch them. They got away lightly at home too when, two days later, the dress was discovered in the wash tub where they had hidden it with a huge burn at the back.

After the furore from the previous week about the fire and damage the older boys had caused, their parents decided that the less said the better and were only too glad to avoid the police knocking at their door. Sylvia was the only one to suffer any consequences of the escapade for the dress was returned to Auntie Ada, who patched it up and sent it back for her to wear again!

The children were frequently left to their own devices, playing in the fields or along the canal with no one apparently concerned for their safety. They were expected to stay out of the way and, as long as they came home by tea time, no one paid them much attention. The canal and railway were unsafe places but the vulnerable children were entirely ignorant of the dangers as they ran wild, always on the look-out for mischief, with Sylvia trailing along. In fact, no one knew where they were most of the time.

PARTING OF THE WAYS

Inevitably there came a time when Sylvia lost interest in playing with the boys in the fields, especially as her mother insisted on her helping out at home. The weight of her domestic responsibilities began to increase, even to the point of her missing out on her schooling.

Sylvia was disheartened by her poor school attendance but it was something over which she had no control because of her mother's ambivalent attitude towards education. In her mother's opinion attending school was not a priority and she kept Sylvia away on the slightest pretext. Sylvia loved school and was eager to learn, so she felt her enforced absence keenly.

Mary would send her daughter to answer the door when the inspector from the School Board called (frequently) regarding Sylvia's poor school attendance, instructing her to say her mother was out. The sympathetic inspector, seeing Sylvia's embarrassment, would reassure her with kindly understanding and leave without challenging her. Sylvia hated telling lies but to her mother it was no big deal.

When it came to the Eleven-Plus Examinations, which determined whether children qualified for high school, Sylvia was warned by her mother not to have ideas about going there. 'It's no use you passing the exam,' she said, 'because we can't afford the uniform.' There was no argument – the matter was closed.

Sylvia was so disappointed. She took the compulsory examination at school with a heavy heart, knowing she was ill-prepared because of her poor standard of education. She knew, too, that her mother would veto her transfer to the high school even if she was successful.

Her best friend passed the examination and happily transferred to Salford's prestigious Pendleton High School for Girls, while Sylvia was left to make the best of things at the secondary modern school, along with all the other failures. Sylvia was envious of her friend, whose parents were able somehow to afford the extra expense. She reasoned that perhaps it was because their family was not as big as hers, but in her heart she knew that her friend's parents' attitude to a good education had a lot to do with it. Her friend soon made new friends and inevitably they drifted apart after a while.

Sylvia knew that even at St Luke's School she could have had a measure of success had her mother allowed her to attend school regularly. However, remaining at St Luke's, a church school, meant that Sylvia would continue to benefit from the daily assemblies that were conducted by the headmaster and attended by the whole school every morning before lessons. The content of the assemblies was entirely Christian, starting and ending with a traditional hymn sung with gusto and enjoyed by the staff and children alike.

This daily routine became a highlight for Sylvia, reassuring her that at least for the next few hours she would be relieved from the responsibilities at home. School was a good place to be; respect and good manners were encouraged by the teachers, in addition to high standards of discipline, giving children the encouragement and support that were generally lacking in the poor community around St Luke's. As well as enjoying her general education, Sylvia loved the weekly visits from the local curate.

Mr Collins, the curate, came from the parish church to the school each week to give religious lessons. He was young, engaging and kind; he obviously cared for the children and loved his vocation. His approach to a subject that was alien to many of his pupils was completely disarming; he made what could have been a difficult and daunting subject interesting and often amusing.

One time he told his class a story about one of the little boys in his Sunday school who went home in tears. When the boy's mother asked him why he was so upset, he explained in his childish manner, 'Mr Collins teached us a song about Jesus.'

His bewildered mother asked, 'Which song did Mr Collins teach you that upset you?'

'Well,' sobbed the little boy, 'he said Jesus wants me to be a sunbeam, but I want to be a train driver!'

Another incident in Mr Collins' Sunday school was over the name Edith. A rather precocious little girl insisted that Edith was a lady in the Bible. The Bible translation used at the time was the King James' Version, written in archaic language using 'thees' and 'thous.' It later turned out that the girl was referring to a story in the New Testament, which stated that Jesus sat with sinners and 'eateth' with them!

What Mr Collins taught about God and the Bible touched the children's hearts and had a great influence on their lives. He told them stories from the Bible, what they meant and how they related to their own lives. For the majority, it was the first time they had heard anything about the Bible or Jesus. Mr Collins brought to life the suffering and the sacrifice of Jesus, the crucifixion, as well as the victory and celebration of the resurrection. He explained God's divine plan of salvation and the importance of receiving forgiveness for sins. Over the many weeks and months that the curate was with them, they learned the simple truths of the Gospel.

Not all the stories he told were from the Bible. One story he called 'The King's Birthday'. The king was to throw a party for his birthday and everybody was invited. Each person was asked to bring a gift in the shape of a container made of gold. Everyone was concerned about the cost of such a gift, exclaiming, 'Gold is so expensive!' Each one thought about what they could bring that would not cost them too much and would only require minimum effort.

One person said, 'I will take him an egg cup.' After this, everyone began to think small. A thimble seemed like a good idea to one, a miniature coffee cup to another and so on.

They set about preparing their tiny gifts and congratulated themselves on their ingenuity, all except for one person who thought, 'The king has shown such kindness to us, I will present him with the biggest and best gift that I can – a bowl of pure gold.'

On the day of the party, everyone arrived with their various containers. One by one they placed their gifts before the king. He gazed at all the gifts arrayed before him then, turning to his guests, he said, 'Pick up your gifts, go into the next room, fill up your containers with diamonds and go home.'

Mr Collins revealed the meaning of the parable, explaining to the children the principles of sowing and reaping: 'As you give, so shall you receive.' He faithfully fulfilled his commission to explain the Gospel to the children and bring the love of God into their lives, showing them how precious they were in God's eyes. He had the ability to make the children feel loved and valued, a concept unfamiliar to Sylvia. He made a great impression on her as she hung on his every word; in years to come, she often reflected on the lasting effect he had had on her and all the children and wondered how many individuals had such a loving and positive effect upon the people they met along the way.

It was Mr Collins who gave her a sense of worth and awakened in her a longing to be loved. During his time with his lively and impressionable charges, he taught them so much about life including the importance of the spoken word and how powerfully they could influence the effect they have on others. It was a lesson she never forgot.

A LOST CHILDHOOD

Sylvia was born into a hand-to-mouth environment. As such, this created a continual struggle for survival for the family, with the children bearing the brunt of their parents' hard and troubled lives. As the arguments and fights increased, the older boys seized the opportunity to escape when they became more independent. They left home one by one, never to return, leaving Sylvia, as the eldest child, with an increased burden of worry and insecurity.

Her younger brothers were more resilient and made themselves scarce when they sensed trouble brewing. Whenever the angry words between her parents escalated into actual fighting, Sylvia would run down the stone steps of the coal cellar, trembling and crying hysterically, praying, 'Please God, stop them!' She tried to block out their loud angry voices, her mother throwing things and her father fending her off. Her mother threw whatever came to hand – on one occasion, a heavy object hit Sylvia's father full in the face and gashed his eye. Sylvia remembered him rushing out of the front door with blood streaming down his face.

Sylvia had to grow up quickly, maturing far beyond her years. So it was that at the age of thirteen she had, out of necessity, taken over much of the responsibility in the home, adapting to her position by becoming more proficient in domestic affairs than her mother. She took on this role in an effort to promote some semblance of order in their chaotic household. Of course, she was too young to shoulder what should have been her parents' responsibilities but there was no alternative, such was the state of their lives.

After school on Fridays, her father's pay day, Sylvia was responsible for collecting the weekly groceries. Her mother would send her, accompanied by one of her younger brothers, to the local Co-op shop about a mile away. They took the baby's pram along to carry back the groceries. Her mother usually gave Sylvia instructions about what to buy, charging her with the responsibility to add one or two extras at her own discretion.

One day Sylvia returned home with the usual groceries with the addition of a large tin of sliced peaches. Unfortunately the bill came to more than she had expected and, when her mother discovered that she had spent all the money, she flew into a rage and struck Sylvia in the face with the back of her hand, knocking her off her feet. Sylvia fell backwards on to the floor and banged her head against the wall.

She wept bitterly, shocked that her mother had struck her so violently; at the same time, she understood that it was the stress that made her mother act in that way. Her mother had not meant to hit her so forcefully, she had just lashed out in the heat of the moment. It took her a while to calm down; Sylvia knew she was sorry but apologies were never expressed in their house.

When Sylvia arrived at school the following Monday, the teachers saw the bruise where her mother's wedding ring had made contact close to her eye. When they asked her about it, Sylvia made some vague excuse for the injury, trying to make light of it. Although the staff were obviously concerned, no action was taken. The small scar remained and was still visible years later. The incident was never mentioned again and Sylvia did not confide in anyone about it.

She felt sorry for her mother, who was more to be pitied than blamed. The family was increasing at a rate faster than her mother could cope with. Young as Sylvia was, she knew that the lack of money and the frequent pregnancies and numerous miscarriages were really the cause of her mother's frustration and violent outbursts.

Over time, it became evident that Sylvia was trapped, a victim of the traditions that dictated a woman's role in the family. Her parents' expectations were governed by ignorance, poverty and their inability to rise above their circumstances. Since she was a girl, it was a given that Sylvia would take on a great deal of the domestic work but, because she was only a child, the weight of responsibility laid on her shoulders was too much to bear. She became resentful and rebellious and dreamed of running away but to no avail. There seemed to be no escape from the same dismal fate as her mother.

But she had a dream, sensing that life was more than the loveless existence and the unrelenting drudgery that was her mother's lot. She was searching, hoping and praying that her miserable situation would change even though there seemed to be no way out. She often thought about the stories the curate had taught them about a loving God; longing for some meaning in her life, she began to look beyond the confines of her home. Maybe somewhere there was a God who loved her. That thought took hold; perhaps there was hope after all.

One night Sylvia had a dream. She was not sure whether she was asleep or awake but it had a profound effect on her. In the dream, she was sitting in the living room; it was very dark and she was alone but unafraid. She looked out of the window into the blackness outside. In the dark sky appeared a cross, hovering and shining iridescently high above the rooftops. It held her gaze as it slowly transformed into a brilliant sword. She felt a distinct sense of reverence, as though she were in the presence of a celestial being.

After a few minutes the vision slowly faded into a gentle mist and disappeared, leaving her with an overwhelming sense of peace and wonder mixed with curiosity about the significance of this extraordinary phenomenon. The experience was so vivid that it remained with her, bringing that same sense of peace and comfort, encouraging her throughout the years ahead when her dreams became a nightmare

Despite her hopes for a better future, Sylvia's prospects of a good education remained severely compromised despite her aptitude for learning. It was not due to the teachers' lack of encouragement – they did their best. The problem lay at home as her mother took every opportunity to keep her away from school to help with the younger siblings or run errands.

Sometimes, when things were desperate and money was short, instead of attending school her mother would send Sylvia on the bus across town to the pawnbroker's shop to pawn her father's suit or some other item of clothing. There was no question of taking anything of real value to pawn as her parents had no jewellery, not even a wristwatch. Added to this, there was the daily, never-ending stream of housework. In her mother's opinion, Sylvia attending school was not a priority; in view of the predicted lifestyle mapped out for her, school was a waste of time.

Sylvia began to reject that lifestyle, however. The world beyond the slums of Salford beckoned and she resolved to escape. She made that important decision one day on her way home from shopping when she was thinking of the depressing direction her life was taking. It was also the day that, on an impulse, she ventured into the public library and a new world of learning opened up to her, igniting a spark of hope.

She began to take every opportunity to read and study. Her Auntie Ada, who worked in the printing trade, readily supplied her with pens, notebooks and copious amounts of surplus stationery. At last Sylvia had found something that lifted her spirits above her hitherto mundane existence. She made notes and read anything and everything that attracted her attention. She was taking the first steps on her escape route and, at the same time, experiencing her first taste of happiness.

Once, as a young teenager, remembering what Mr Collins the curate had taught them about the power of words, Sylvia became engaged in a conversation with some school friends about the importance of the words we speak. They were discussing the saying 'Sticks and stones will break my bones but names will never hurt me'. Although uneducated in worldly or philosophical matters, Sylvia voiced her doubts about that saying. She did not think it was a valid argument. As youngsters, they were exploring and questioning the things they had been taught and she felt that this was a really important subject, even though she could not understand or explain the reason behind her conviction. She remarked that she believed that words were important and that one day we would all have to give an account of every word we had ever spoken. She surprised herself, not for believing it but for actually voicing it. She knew instinctively that it was an amazing concept and, even though she had no idea where the thought had come from, her increasing interest in the words we speak and their spiritual power continued to develop and hold her attention.

Her avid reading led her to a passage in the Bible and the words spoken by Jesus: 'For every idle word men shall speak, they will give account of it on the day of judgement, for by your words you will be justified and by your words you will be condemned.' Those words lined up with the intriguing psychological concept of mind over matter, the power of thoughts and their connection. Today medical science is advancing in understanding how the content and quality of our thoughts, and consequently our words, affects our health and well-being for better or worse.

OPPORTUNITY KNOCKS

Sylvia left school at the age of fifteen and started work at the huge Co-operative Wholesale Society (CWS) headquarters in Balloon Street in Manchester as a junior filing clerk in the sales and advertising department.

Her new colleagues collectively took her under their wing and were immensely supportive. Having witnessed her arrival as a naive, unworldly schoolgirl, they nurtured her and introduced her to the real world. Under their friendly influence, Sylvia's horizons widened. She was gradually coaxed out of her inferiority complex and persuaded to accompany them to CWS social events and even to join the choir.

Sometimes at the weekends they went to the speedway races at the Manchester BelleVue speedway stadium. On other occasions she was delighted to be invited to join in hiking around Hayfield, Edale and Kinder Scout with the vibrant group of young people in her section. They organised outings, took her to the theatre and showed her how to laugh, joke and enjoy life. It was her first taste of approval and acceptance, a wonderful and liberating experience.

With time, Sylvia could have been happy there and progressed well in the company but the life of commerce was not for her. She still wanted to be a nurse! She was just waiting for the opportunity.

It was not long before opportunity came knocking at Sylvia's door when she heard that the local hospitals were introducing a nursing cadet scheme. So, at the age of sixteen, despite her mother's opposition and rigid hold over her, she took her first step towards realizing her dream with the support of her long-suffering father. She enrolled in the pre-nursing scheme at Hope Hospital in Salford, the place that had been the focus of her aspirations to become a nurse for as long as she could remember.

When she announced to her colleagues at the CWS that her application had been successful, the 'Balloon Street Gang' rallied round. Within a few weeks, on the day she left, they waved her goodbye not only with their good wishes but also with an abundance of gifts suitable for a young lady setting out to pursue her dream. They were proud of the part they had played in Sylvia's transformation, and rightly so. It was due to them that her low self-esteem had given way to a new-found boldness, enabling her to venture out into her new life confidently. She was laden with their parting gifts – a smart black patent-leather handbag, leather gloves, silk scarf and an umbrella. They were luxuries far beyond her wildest dreams!

More than the gifts, their kind regard and approval were priceless. Thanks to them, Sylvia had arrived like Cinderella and left like a princess! Because of them, she began to accept a sense of worth. It was as if they had taken the pieces of her poverty-stricken mentality and, with their love and encouragement, enabled her to hold up her head and look the world in the eye. Although it took some time for her deep-seated inferiority complex to disappear completely, her fears and anxiety gradually gave way to a new and more accepting self-image.

In the weeks prior to the start of the cadet scheme, Sylvia was in a constant state of excitement. On the first day her joy knew no bounds as she joined the group of new students assembled in the lecture room for their induction at the hospital.

There were four hospitals in the cadet scheme; each student would spend approximately two-and-a-half years moving between the hospitals and departments every few months. The programme was established to equip them with a good working knowledge of hospital life and prepare them for a nursing career. Each student would be assigned to a department in one of the hospitals three days a week, returning to the training school with the rest of the class for lectures for the two remaining days. They were off duty at the weekends.

The two days of lectures were a saving grace for Sylvia because she was acutely aware of the deficiencies in her education and general knowledge; most of the time she felt like she was playing 'catch up'.

Of course they were not permitted to work on the wards but that did not concern Sylvia. Simply being allowed to work in any of the various hospital departments was fulfilling enough. She was thrilled with the standard, plain, uninspiring beige overall she was required to wear and even more excited about the 'real' nurse's cap, which for her was an added bonus. She was in her element and so proud whenever an unsuspecting visitor stopped her in a corridor and asked her for directions, addressing her as 'Nurse!'.

Although only a sixteen-year-old cadet, Sylvia was undoubtedly on the first rung of her nursing career. Even though it was not strictly a nursing position, it was the most significant thing that had ever happened to her. She proudly announced the details of her first hospital placement to her family and anyone else who would listen, naively declaring that she was ready for anything! The wide world beckoned. She did not stop to consider that there might be some serious challenges for her to face along the way.

Sylvia was soon to discover that, over the next two and a half years and moving between various departments as a cadet, some placements would be more memorable than others. The most dramatic and shocking experience of all was her first assignment at the Manchester Skin Hospital. You could say she was thrown in at the deep end.

She had no idea what to expect and set out on that first day in nervous anticipation as she travelled on the bus into Manchester. It was still quite dark and she was surrounded by preoccupied passengers heading out of Salford into the city.

She was, without doubt, the most excited passenger on the bus that morning!

Arriving at the Skin Hospital, Sylvia hesitated, awestruck at the sight of the imposing Victorian building beckoning her in. The hospital stood opposite the equally grand Manchester Opera House, the two buildings dominating the other buildings in the busy crowded street. The wide stone steps at the front of the hospital led up to a large ornate door.

Nervously, she entered the public reception area that opened into a huge hall with a high ceiling and row upon row of benches, seating what looked like hundreds of people. This, Sylvia supposed, must be the waiting room for the outpatients department. She turned back to the entrance, trying to decide which of the several closed doors she should enter. In a weird sort of way, she felt like Alice in Wonderland, opening one door after another, but after she had peered inside several doors something told her that this was no Wonderland! Shivering involuntarily, her sense of wonder gave way to a feeling of dread and foreboding.

Eventually she located the matron's office and reported for duty. The matron scrutinised Sylvia with her critical eye and ordered her wait while she summoned a nurse to escort her to the nurses' changing room to put on her cadet uniform and cap. Her excitement and anticipation returned once she had put on her uniform, making her feel like a 'real nurse' once again. She announced to the waiting escort that she was ready to go!

The rest of the day was like no other Sylvia had ever experienced. She was shown around the stark clinical departments where doctors and nurses worked with impersonal efficiency. In the consulting rooms and cubicles, she was subjected to the most shocking sights: skin diseases of every description; rashes and blemishes; disfigured faces; putrid and foul-smelling leg ulcers, and several pitiful conditions that revealed humanity at its ugliest and most degraded. The heat and smell in each department was so nauseating that Sylvia struggled to suppress her urge to retch.

The nurse in charge of her induction hurried her along as she explained everything in a matter-of-fact manner as though this grim depressing environment were normal, barely noticing Sylvia's increasing horror. Eventually, having done the rounds, she took her to the nurses' refectory.

As Sylvia drank a cup of tea, the nurse sat down opposite her and studied her enquiringly, as though expecting some response, but Sylvia's mind was reeling and she could not think of anything to say. Mistaking her silence for intelligence, the nurse assumed that the induction had gone well and indicated that it was time to move on.

They negotiated a few more corridors and ended up in the leg-ulcer clinic where Sylvia was to work. The nurse briskly handed her over to the sister-in-charge who unceremoniously handed Sylvia a bucket and instructed her to collect the soiled dressings from the patients waiting to be seen by the doctor. Unlike the strict hygienic procedures in clinics today, she was not given any forceps, protective clothing or gloves to wear. All the staff were so busy that they just left her to get on with it! She had the distinct impression that she was in their way and supervising her was something they could well do without.

After what seemed like an eternity, a nurse was delegated to escort Sylvia to lunch. By this time, due to the overwhelming heat and smell, Sylvia was close to fainting and grateful to be relieved of her duties. But when they reached the dining room much to everyone's disgust at the sight of the food she was violently sick. So without more ado, they sent her home!

Following a restless night filled with horrendous nightmares, Sylvia returned to the hospital the next day. Over the next few weeks, she gradually became accustomed to the awful sights, sounds and smells. By the time she left three months later, she managed to eat her lunch every day quite happily!

Subsequent placements introduced Sylvia to other hospitals and various departments but none of them were as shocking as that first experience at the Skin Hospital, although some time later she did manage a spectacular fainting episode in the kitchen at Hope Hospital where the overwhelming heat and smell affected her once again. However, in that instance it was just the smell of fish and chips!

EDNA AND MR TEXAS

It was during Sylvia's time as a first-year nursing cadet that a very significant event took place apart from her nursing experiences. This was to change the direction of her life completely. Looking back, she was able to trace the influences on her life that brought her closer to that event.

The care and attention Sylvia had received from her Auntie Ada when she was a child, and Ada's substantial contribution to her upbringing, saved Sylvia from the more traumatic effects of her dysfunctional family. Furthermore, the support and encouragement of the teachers at her school inspired her, despite her many disadvantages. Later, Sylvia was encouraged by the unforgettable and significant introduction to spiritual matters by Mr Collins, the curate. Eventually, when she left school, she was influenced by the wonderful group of CWS colleagues who befriended her and raised her sights, helping her to see the world in a new light.

Her gradual progress eventually brought her to the turning point in her life. It was on one of Sylvia's placements as a first-year cadet nurse at Hope Hospital that she met Edna, a remarkable lady who worked in the medical records office.

This lovely lady took a particular interest in Sylvia and her cadet friend, Clare. She made them the subject of her prayers and subsequently invited them to her home for tea one Sunday afternoon when there was a Billy Graham film being shown at her church. Although they had vaguely heard of the American evangelist Billy Graham, they were not interested enough to go along to a church to see a film about him. Not to be thwarted, and anticipating their response, Edna also invited two young soldiers who were billeted in the barracks in Manchester. That did the trick – all of a sudden the girls were interested!

During tea at Edna's home Sylvia and Clare did their best to outdo each other in trying to impress the very polite and reserved young men and showed a great interest in going to the church with them after tea. (Incidentally, Clare made such a good impression that she eventually ended up marrying one of them!) To Sylvia's surprise, the Elim Pentecostal Church was nothing like the serious, disciplined services in the Church of England that she had been accustomed to during her schooldays. This church was alive with inspiring hymns and cheerful choruses. The film, *Mr Texas*, was so riveting that it held their attention throughout, as did the brief sermon by the pastor afterwards. He expounded upon the theme of the film, challenging them to consider its message of the love of God. That night, Sylvia made the decision to become a Christian, a major turning point in her life.

The following days and weeks were a whirlwind of new experiences and discoveries. She was surrounded by young enthusiastic Christians and she joined them wholeheartedly. She heard new songs and 'modern' hymns that were popular at that time during the Billy Graham London Crusades, which contrasted with the traditions and solemn hymns she had been familiar with in the Church of England. She joined a Bible class and was baptised in water as a witness to her new-found faith. She began to learn things about the Christian faith that she had never known before. At last she had met the God who loved her!

She faced ridicule and disbelief from her family and friends. Her mother, in particular, tried to prevent Sylvia from attending what she called 'that new-fangled church' and objected to her association with her new Christian friends, but it soon became obvious that her hold over Sylvia was beginning to lose its grip.

Sylvia began to enjoy life. She was no longer fearful or held down by a sense of inferiority and happily made it to the end of the cadet scheme, gratified by her success.

ADVENTURES OF A STUDENT NURSE

At the age of eighteen, Sylvia joined eleven other student nurses in the preliminary training school at Hope Hospital in Salford. She spent the next three and a half years fulfilling her dream. Despite the many challenges along the way, she never had any doubts or regrets; becoming a nurse was what she wanted to do more than anything else and she was well on the way to accomplishing it. In caring for the sick and vulnerable, she began to understand the meaning of compassion. Her rough edges gave way to a gentler side to her nature and, over the course of her training, she began to appreciate the universal need to love and be loved.

At the start of their training, student nurses were required to live in the nurses' home situated in the hospital grounds. For Sylvia, the transition from her poor, overcrowded home life to the impressive nurses' home with luxuries she had only dreamed of was a wonderful experience. At last she was free from the poor lifestyle she was accustomed to.

She revelled in the freedom and independence of living in the nurses' home. And what a home it was! She had a lovely bedroom all to herself, spotlessly clean and centrally heated – in her view, it was the height of luxury. There were several huge bathrooms along the corridor and a hand basin with hot water in her bedroom. Maids cleaned the rooms and changed the bed linen and towels every week. Sylvia marvelled at the splendid long corridor outside the bedrooms with its magnificently polished floor. It was like heaven! She had never been in a hotel but imagined that even a hotel could not have been more sumptuous!

The nurses' dining room, situated below them on the ground floor, was large and awe-inspiring with a designated seating arrangement. The first-year students were allocated places at the front of the room under the watchful eye of the home sister, who served their meals and scrutinised what they were eating. At the far end was the staff-nurses' section with waitress service. The ward sisters had their own private dining room away from the rest of the staff. New students soon learned that where they ate their meals was not negotiable; woe betide anyone who thought otherwise!

There were quite a few rules to be observed by the students living in the nurses home, one of which was the 10pm curfew, which was generally ignored. A number of the students quickly learned the art of climbing in through windows late at night!

The four male nurses had separate accommodation. They had the advantage over the rest of the class as they were two years into their training for their mental-health qualification. They were seconded from Manchester to join the nurses at Hope Hospital to complete their general nursing experience. They brought with them an annoying sense of superiority but, having been raised with six brothers, Sylvia thought she had the measure of boys.

However, unlike her brothers, Sylvia found these young men to be attractive and exciting and soon discovered the charms of male attention! So when one of them offered to help her with her homework one evening and invited himself to her room, she was flattered at his kind offer. Much to her surprise, when she mentioned this invitation to her girlfriend, the latter, who was obviously more worldly wise, was horrified. She took Sylvia aside and explained that the young man in question had intentions that were far from brotherly!

When Sylvia realised that her male colleagues saw her as a simpleton, she determined not to let them get the better of her. She resolved to prove to them that, although they may have viewed her as an innocent abroad both socially and emotionally when she arrived, she would match them in the classroom any day! She was spurred on to put greater effort into her studies; subsequently, when the final hospital examination results were published at the end of the year, she had excelled way beyond her expectations, matching the results of her more experienced male colleagues – much to their annoyance and her delight!

The first year flew by in a whirlwind of new and exciting experiences, interspersed with challenges every time the students were transferred to a new ward. It was generally accepted that the ward sisters made it their mission to instil fear into every new intake of junior nurses. There was one surprising exception – Sister Hudson. She ruled the children's ward with a rod of iron but her severe exterior concealed a heart of gold. She loved the children in her care and instilled that love in her students. However, she was not without a few eccentricities. Woe betide anyone who attempted to leave the ward after their night shift without making sure that all the knives, forks and spoons were lined up on the kitchen counter, present and correct for her inspection when she came on duty each morning! There were other ward sisters who had their own particular idiosyncrasies too but, by the end of their first year, the students had learned not to be intimidated so easily.

FIRST NIGHT DUTY

As the students approached the end of an exciting and exhausting first year, they received news that they were due for night duty. Having worked on the wards and alternated with their studies in the training school during their first year, this would be a leap into unknown territory.

They had no experience of working at night. Rumours abounded with stories of what to expect, with a number of senior nurses taking a perverse delight in trying to scare them and often succeeding! Some of the warnings were realistic but most of the stories were aimed at the nervous students' overactive imaginations, particularly the warnings to look out for 'the lady in grey' or, more precisely, 'the nurse in grey' who it was claimed walked the dark corridors at night!

In due course, the anticipated list went up on the noticeboard with the names of the students selected for night duty for the next three months. Sylvia, along with the rest of her class, gathered around the board searching for her name with a mixture of hope and dread. Manoeuvring herself to the front of the group, she saw her name listed to start night duty the following week. She was ridiculously excited, exhilarated and terrified – all at the same time!

She dragged herself away from the noticeboard and reported for duty that morning, all the time preoccupied with the dreaded prospect of being on a ward at night. She was heading towards the unknown, unsure of how she would cope.

Sylvia's first night on duty proved to be a memorable one. She nervously presented herself a little before 8pm on the ward she had been assigned to. It was a women's medical ward, with twenty beds lined up in rows of ten along each side of the long room. She followed the rest of the night-staff team as they joined the day staff in the sister's office to receive the ward report. The handover was taking place during the evening visiting time.

Sylvia listened intently to the sister's report outlining the details of each patient's condition and treatment. Although she was impressed by all the important information, as the newest and most junior nurse she knew she would not be expected to take much responsibility for the patients' care during the course of the night; she only hoped she would be up to whatever would be asked of her. She was eager to please and to show that she could be relied upon, whatever the task.

The first duty Sylvia was entrusted with that night as they left the sister's office was to collect the flowers from the ward. It was the custom in those days to remove the flowers each evening – something to do with carbon dioxide, she thought. Although nervous about venturing alone into the ward while the visitors were still there, she walked calmly down its length to the sluice at the far end, conscious of the curious gaze of the patients and their visitors following her. Reaching the sluice, she pulled out a trolley and proceeded back into the ward. She began to gather the various flower arrangements from the patients' bedsides, placing them carefully onto the trolley. Manoeuvring the trolley was not as easy as it looked; apparently there was a technique to trolley management that she was yet to learn, evidenced by the fact that the wheels on this particular contraption were destined to operate individually in opposing directions!

Nervous and self-conscious, she struggled with increasing difficulty as the trolley rattled along noisily. She tried to give the impression that she was completely in control and unperturbed despite her burning cheeks.

After circumnavigating the farthest reaches of the ward, which in these circumstances appeared to be particularly vast, she was finishing her round and heading for the safety of the sluice when one of the vases toppled over, spilling water and crashing to the floor. In her panic, Sylvia lunged forward and tried to catch it. As she slipped on the wet floor, she grabbed the trolley and pulled it over on top of herself with a tremendous crash. Humiliated and embarrassed, she scrambled in an to her feet, dripping wet and covered in flowers, foliage and confusion!

She could not recall what happened next, apart from the unforgettable sight of the Sister standing at the end of the ward hands on hips with a look of utter disbelief on her face. It was the first of Sylvia's night duty blunders but not the last!

LOVE LAUGHTER AND MISTAKES!

The next two and a half years passed by at an astonishing speed. With each successive year, the class of student nurses became more confident and skilful, and many significant occasions and memorable experiences enriched their lives. There was laughter as well as tears along the way, with some spectacular incidents punctuating the strict, disciplined routines.

Falling in love with a handsome charge nurse was one of Sylvia's early romantic episodes; fortunately, it didn't end in tears! There were many moments etched forever in her memory, like the night she allowed the porridge pan to dry out on the stove in the ward kitchen causing a mighty explosion and scattering porridge everywhere, including the ceiling.

On another occasion, as a more senior nurse on night duty, she was assigned to one of the first wards she had worked on as a first-year nurse. Back then she had been intimidated by the senior ward orderly, who had not taken kindly to young nurses usurping her unquestioned authority, making things as difficult as possible for the new and inexperienced nurses. Sylvia had been terrified of her! This time, as the senior nurse in charge of the ward, she was more experienced and faced her nemesis, Freda the orderly, with confidence, making it quite clear that this time she was in charge. Having asserted her authority, she gave the staff, including Freda, their duties for the evening as they prepared to settle the twenty-two elderly female patients for the night.

Although Sylvia was the senior nurse in charge, if the opportunity arose she was always willing to be 'hands on' when it came to the more routine tasks that she enjoyed. So on that first night, she joined the other nurses in the dimly-lit ward and began to help settle down the patients for the night. Some of the patients were confused and anxious but a few calming words as she tucked them in helped them to relax.

One dear lady, glad of the attention and quite talkative, introduced herself as Betty. She offered a sweet from a bag she held out to Sylvia. Usually it was the rule for the nurses to accept sweets from patients and put them in their pocket to be disposed of discreetly later. However, at Betty's insistence and seeing that the sweets were wrapped, Sylvia took one and popped it into her mouth as they chatted quietly until her new friend became drowsy and ready for sleep.

Soon all the patients had settled down and some of the nurses gathered briefly with the orderlies, including Freda, in the ward kitchen for a cup of tea. Until that point, Freda had shown no inclination to make conversation with Sylvia. To her surprise, as Freda walked into the kitchen she asked Sylvia if she had been offered a sweet by Betty.

'Yes,' Sylvia replied, adding quickly, 'it's OK, the toffee was wrapped'

With a malicious gleam in her eye, Freda responded, 'Well, it so happens that Betty sucks her sweets then wraps them up again!'

Touché! Another lesson learned!

There were many occasions working on the wards that Sylvia remembered fondly – and there were many too hard to forget!

MOVING ON

Soon it was time to consider moving on. Near the end of their training, the class, who had become like family and formed strong friendships, began to consider their future as fully-trained State Registered Nurses. For some, the hospital had become a second home and, despite the harsh and disciplined lifestyle, they all cherished the experience of living and working together. It was with some sadness that they began to speculate about what would be their next move.

The final examinations were over and the results were due any day. Sylvia and her friends were anticipating the next exciting step in their nursing career. Until then, apart from the small contingent of Irish students, few of them had ventured much beyond Salford. Now the world was their oyster and they were ready to take full advantage of every opportunity. They were preparing to follow the tradition of newly qualified nurses at that time to move on to midwifery training, apart from the male nurses who returned to their Manchester training school. Most of the Irish nurses left for their homes back in Ireland. Only a handful of the other students, mostly local girls, remained.

One evening, Sylvia and her three friends gathered in her bedroom in the nurses' home to discuss their choices for midwifery training. They each had ideas of the most interesting place to train; after much debate, and without the advantage of the internet, of course, they narrowed it down to three places: Harrogate, Lancaster and London.

Although they were good friends and had enjoyed living and training together in Salford, they were ready for a change. That change did not include either Lancaster or Harrogate for Sylvia. The others were north-bound while she had set her sights on London.

'Why London?' they chorused.

'I'm going to find a husband,' was her not-entirely flippant reply!

Choosing to move to London was not an altogether random or frivolous decision for Sylvia. She had recently been introduced to a midwife who was visiting Salford on her travels as a prominent speaker in the Salvation Army. She had trained at the Salvation Army Mothers' Hospital in Hackney and highly recommended the training school there. It was with her encouragement that Sylvia, eager to train at a Christian hospital, decided to apply for a place. However, it turned out that her assumption was misplaced; she was yet to discover that, even with the best intentions, she did not always make the best choices and often made very unwise decisions.

In May 1958, Sylvia bade farewell to her friends and left Salford for London, delighted to have been given a place at the Salvation Army Mothers' Hospital in Hackney. On the first day of her midwifery training she joined the new intake of pupil midwives, ready for the next important stage of her career.

Since it was a Salvation Army Hospital, she had naively expected a warm and friendly welcome but she was soon to learn that working in a Christian hospital did not guarantee Christian virtues. In fact, almost as soon as she opened her mouth Sylvia was singled out by the staff nurse in charge of the new recruits. It appeared that the staff nurse had decided that Sylvia's broad Lancashire accent was a sure sign of ignorance. She inferred that Sylvia couldn't possibly be a qualified State Registered Nurse and certainly, in her opinion, did not have the makings of a trained midwife! She made no secret of her unfriendly attitude towards Sylvia and proceeded to make things as difficult for her as possible.

Initially the staff nurse managed to dampen Sylvia's fervour and for a while her enthusiasm faltered under her constant harassment. But it did not take Sylvia long to realise that she had a battle on her hands; she toughened up and, thanks to the staff nurse's hostile attitude, she learned some valuable lessons – most of which had nothing to do with delivering babies!

The hospital had originally started as a Salvation Army outreach for single mothers in the poor communities in the East End of London prior to the outbreak of the Second World War. The hospital was close to Bethnal Green, an area that had endured more than its share of the horrors of the war. As Sylvia became familiar with the area, she was saddened to learn of the hardships suffered by the East Enders during the air raids.

One of the most shocking things she learned of was the incident on March 3, 1943, remembered as 'The Bethnal Green Tube Station Disaster'. It was a defining moment in the history of the East End. Nearly two thousand residents slept on the platforms of the tube station each night during the Blitz as London experienced the full blast of enemy bombs. On that particular night, the warning siren alerted the residents of a feared attack. As people fled to find shelter in the tube station, a woman tripped and fell down the steps leading to the platform. A domino effect then sent hundreds of frantic people toppling over each other; 173 people were killed in that incident. It wasn't until after the war that the details of the tube-station disaster were made public; it was decided at the time to withhold broadcasting the news in the interests of public morale.

The East End was still bearing the scars of the war in the 1950s when Sylvia arrived as a pupil midwife. She encountered the hardships of those living in the community around the Mothers' Hospital, similar to the stories viewed on the popular television programme entitled *Call the Midwife* in more recent times.

Being a pupil midwife proved to be quite a challenge, especially when Sylvia discovered that babies did not always arrive when expected! To fulfil the number of births necessary for her training records, she was required to deliver ten babies under supervision within the first few weeks. This meant taking her turn at being 'on call' on several nights. Instead of retiring to bed and being dragged out to attend to a mother due to give birth, Sylvia spent her 'on call' time fully dressed in her uniform, lying on her bed, waiting to be called to attend any mother due to give birth that night. It was not a good decision and before long she was compelled to give up the idea. She was constantly tired after a few such nights of awaiting deliveries and then having to fulfil her regular day shift,

One of the most satisfying customs at the Mothers' Hospital was the prayer of thanksgiving by the midwife and the new mother for the safe delivery of the baby. It was a privilege to share such an important and often emotional moment with the mother. The request was never refused and the nurses never took the birth of a healthy new baby for granted.

DARK DAYS IN DAGENHAM

After six months training in the hospital, pupil midwives were sent out to work in the community where they were each assigned to a district midwife who would oversee the next phase of their training. Sylvia was to stay with a midwife in Dagenham but, just a few days before she was due to leave, she went down with flu and was confined to bed.

When the senior nurse responsible for the students' community experience heard that Sylvia was unwell, she sent a porter to her room with a bottle of Lucozade and instructions to relocate to Dagenham immediately, with advice to wear a mask! Still feverish and feeling very unwell, Sylvia dutifully travelled across London by bus to her next assignment.

On arrival at the address in Dagenham, she was greeted by the elderly district midwife. Although she noted Sylvia's feverish appearance, she was equally unsympathetic. She took Sylvia out on her rounds almost as soon as she arrived, intending to take full advantage of her young assistant.

She had planned for Sylvia to do most of the visits before and after the home deliveries and was not at all impressed when Sylvia confessed that she could not ride a bike. Obviously irritated, the district midwife instructed her to practise cycling outside in the street until she could ride the bike without falling off. She made it clear that she expected Sylvia to be able to accomplish her duties using the bicycle, despite her feeble protests.

Within a few days, the midwife had delegated the majority of her home visits to Sylvia who was not only very unwell but was expected to fulfil her duties on a bike she had not been able ride two days earlier! The district midwife sent Sylvia out on her own, still trying to master the bike while balancing her nurse's black bag at the front and a large brown paper bag containing a metal bedpan clanking loudly at the rear.

Incredibly, the midwife insisted on sending Sylvia on home visits despite her obvious symptoms of infection, disregarding the welfare of the mothers and their babies. Sylvia found this negligent attitude very disturbing and she lay awake at night wondering what she should do. In those days, students did not challenge their superiors.

Added to this dilemma, riding the bike on her daily rounds was a nightmare! She frequently returned from her visits with her legs bruised, bleeding or covered in oil, not to mention with her stockings torn.

All things considered, it did not take Sylvia long to come to the conclusion that she was not destined to be a district midwife! She hated it.

Then came the final straw: the day when she careered out of control down a steep busy main road in Dagenham town centre aptly called Devil's Hill. In absolute panic she approached the traffic lights at a major junction, knowing that if the signal turned red she would, without doubt, be unable to stop and would probably fall off – or worse!

Miraculously, she made it through the junction and raced at high speed until she crashed the bike outside the house she had been heading towards 'as a matter of urgency', only to find that the doctor had already arrived. He was sitting beside the newly delivered mother and her baby, chatting and smoking a cigar. 'Carry on, nurse,' he said, blowing smoke in her face as he rose from his chair and departed.

Later that day, after much soul searching and feeling completely depressed and deflated, Sylvia wrote to Barbara, her friend in Salford. During their general nursing training, Barbara had suggested that they travel abroad and work in the USA once they had qualified. Sylvia now agreed with her. To her dismay, Barbara replied within a few days informing her that she had changed her mind as she was now engaged to be married! However, Barbara or no Barbara, Sylvia knew she could no longer stay in a situation that made her so unhappy.

In desperation, she contacted the matron at her old hospital in Salford and asked her if she could have her job back as a staff nurse. To Sylvia's relief and delight, the matron agreed to her request. She promptly handed in her notice at the Mothers' Hospital and packed her bags, ready to depart at the earliest opportunity. She was relieved at the prospect of returning to Salford. She needed time to think and plan her next move.

Before returning to Salford, she reviewed her progress with a sense of satisfaction despite this recent setback. Lying in bed early one morning, she considered her accomplishments so far. 'My nursing career has taken me through many challenges already,' she told herself. 'But, by the grace of God, I have successfully qualified as a State Registered Nurse. On many occasions my successes have been hard won. I remember the time when a test paper was returned to me by my tutor with the stern exasperated reproof, "Nurse, your spelling is atrocious!" At least the content of my paper was acceptable.' Sylvia smiled. 'Even if my spelling was not.'

She continued to encourage herself. 'No one knows the uphill climb I endured to achieve my nursing qualification and no one could be more proud of their success than I am. Despite such obvious shortcomings, against all the odds here I am – a fully-trained nurse. I accomplished that even with the disadvantage of my poor education and without the benefit of a stable or loving family to encourage me.'

Desire and determination drove Sylvia on; even in her weakest moments, she had never doubted that one day she would fulfil her dream. She was happy to be going back home, having secured a new position as a staff nurse at Hope Hospital where she hoped she would have the space to take stock while gaining more experience in general nursing.

However, before leaving London and the Mothers' Hospital, there was one more significant event that was to change the direction of Sylvia's life forever.

ROMANCE IN THE AIR

Having decided that she was not destined to become a midwife, Sylvia set her sights on furthering her career back home in Lancashire but, before leaving London, she had to serve the one-month notice period at the Mothers' Hospital. During that time she continued to enjoy the benefits of being a pupil midwife at the hospital.

One benefit was the occasional donation of complimentary tickets to the shows at various London theatres and the Royal Albert Hall for the Proms, besides invitations from Christian organisations. It was a concert one Saturday night at the Methodist Central Hall that proved to be a turning point. The students of the London Elim Bible College were the hosts that evening and made the contingent of young pupil midwives very welcome.

After the concert, the Bible College students and the pupil midwives congregated on the pavement outside the hall, losing no time in getting to know each other. Above the animated conversations in a variety of accents, a distinctive Lancashire strain caught Sylvia's attention; it was like music to her ears. Was that the sound of Salford?

The source of the familiar accent was a tall, dark and handsome young man with a friendly smile. They made their introductions and before long were engaged in conversation about their respective home towns. Sylvia learned that the young man's name was Steve and that he came from Wigan, which was about an hour's bus journey from her home in Salford. Eventually the students and the pupil midwives dispersed. Together with her nurse companions, all in high spirits, Sylvia made her way back to the Mothers' Hospital.

To her surprise, Sylvia's new admirer turned up the next morning at the Elim Church in Leyton, the place where she worshipped. Thus began a delightful series of dates across

London, meeting whenever they could between Steve's studies and Sylvia's midwifery duties. She was even invited as Steve's guest to tea one weekend at the Bible College, where she was the centre of the students' attention and speculation!

As she had already decided to leave the Mothers' Hospital, and being absolutely resolute, Sylvia served her notice period and prepared to return to Salford just as their friendship started to progress. Their subsequent courtship was a long-distance affair but their relationship blossomed as they maintained contact by public telephone as often as they could. As Sylvia was living and working in Salford, they met only at the end of the Bible College terms either in Salford or Wigan. Their meetings were shorter now and regulated by the time available in between travelling and family commitments. They were never alone for long, as friends and family members claimed their attention.

Herein lay the source of Sylvia and Steve's complex and, at times, incomprehensible relationship. It did not develop as Sylvia had expected. Due to the constraints of time and opportunity, they were unwittingly establishing a superficial and shallow relationship. Sylvia reassured herself that in time, in a more favourable environment and given the right circumstances, their romance would blossom. As a result, she fell in love with love and ignored the signs of incompatibility, dismissing any doubts she had and making allowances for the differences in their personalities. She was looking at the situation through rose-tinted glasses and missed all the warning signs.

MEETING THE OPPOSITION

Meeting Steve's family – and his mother in particular – was not at all what Sylvia had anticipated. As they arrived at his home in Wigan for the first time, Steve looked anxiously at her and asked, 'Are you nervous?'

Somewhat surprised,Sylvia replied, 'No, not at all.' Although slightly perplexed, she cheerfully followed him into the house to meet the family who were obviously expecting them.

Much to her dismay, she soon understood why Steve was so anxious. There was no warmth in their greeting; although they were polite, they were strangely reserved. The atmosphere in the house was strained, making Sylvia feel uncomfortable. She found Steve's mother's manner especially unwelcoming. She had the distinct impression that something was wrong and that his mother was not happy with the situation. Sensing his mother's barely concealed antagonism, thoughts of Daniel in the lion's den flitted across Sylvia's mind!

Sylvia was puzzled at the time but later learned that his mother had warned Steve at the beginning of his course at the Bible College that, should he become distracted by a girlfriend, she would withdraw his allowance. It seemed remarkably unreasonable to Sylvia but there was little she could do about it. Their long-distance relationship continued despite Steve's mother's disapproval, and eventually they became engaged to be married.

True to her word, his mother stopped the allowance Steve needed to continue his theological studies at the Bible College. She announced this decision to her son. Despite the fact that Sylvia was engaged to him, she did not include her in the conversation; in fact, she ignored Sylvia and inferred that it was none of her business!

Sylvia was shocked to witness the woman's draconian attitude towards her eldest son who was dependent on her support. Despite this, the young couple had no intention of changing their plans. Undeterred, they decided that Sylvia would provide Steve with the finances necessary to complete his studies during his final year at college until he started earning a salary following his graduation.

As a probationer pastor with the Elim Church, Steve was required to apply for permission to marry. He discovered that he would have to wait two years before permission was granted. Although this caused much frustration, they agreed to wait so that he could complete his training. This would also give them plenty of time to plan their wedding! In the meantime, Sylvia moved in with her friend in Salford and continued working as a staff nurse at Hope Hospital. When the opportunity arose, she added to her nursing qualifications by training to become a health visitor, another accomplishment of which she was immensely proud.

The run-up to the wedding was mostly a one-sided affair as Steve, having completed his training, was now a probationer minister at a church in London. Sylvia, with the help of her friends, made all the arrangements for the wedding which was to take place in Salford. None of their parents were actively involved in the wedding plans.

Looking back, it was a most peculiar situation. Steve was away in London and quite happy to let Sylvia make all the arrangements. The long-distance relationship made her feel uneasy at times, as if the distance between them was more than the miles that separated them. However, she enjoyed planning the wedding, was more than happy to take care of all the arrangements and carried on regardless.

SARAH'S STORY

It wasn't only Sylvia who was having doubts about their relationship; Steve's mother, Sarah, was becoming increasingly concerned. From an early age she had known that something was wrong with Steve. Even as a child, he had been unlike her other three children in many ways. She often thought of how unresponsive he was and how reluctant he was to engage with the normal everyday family life that the other children enjoyed.

For twenty-two years she had kept her worries and fears to herself; now, despite every effort to keep him on the straight and narrow, she was about to lose control. She would have to let go and the very prospect filled her with dread.

She was used to organising and regulating every aspect of Steve's life. For the most part he had been an easy child to manage, passive and compliant; as a teenager, the quality of his life had depended on the strict routine she had imposed. She had managed to keep him on an even keel, ensuring that he did not deviate from what she considered were his best interests. It was an arrangement that had worked well – until now.

Living in accommodation behind the dry-cleaning shop where Sarah worked as a manager enabled her to keep an eye on him when he was at home, and her constant surveillance went unnoticed. Even when the shop was closed on Sundays, she maintained her control over Steve when the family went to church together.

Over the years, Sarah had kept her concerns regarding Steve's behaviour and development to herself. If it ever crossed her mind that there might have been some help for him, she dismissed it. After all, he was no trouble; she could handle him even though his odd behaviour bewildered her at times. He was occasionally stubborn and uncooperative, but he was not rebellious. Sometimes he helped his father with his waste-paper business in the property next door but otherwise he was content to stay indoors. As a child, although he got on well with his brothers and sister, he preferred to play quietly by himself. He was average in his schoolwork but did not make friends easily; being on his own suited him.

As a young boy, Sarah had encouraged him, as she did with all her children, to become independent and self-reliant. He never took the initiative, preferring to follow what everyone else was doing. She wondered if he was just lazy and often rebuked him for what she considered to be his indolence. All the care and attention she had invested in raising him seemed unrewarded as he showed her little affection. She watched him grow into an isolated teenager with few friends and little interest in the world around him.

At the age of eighteen Steve learned to drive. Having found something that awakened his interest, he became obsessed with all things mechanical. He found a job as a delivery van driver for Lyons, the confectioners, which he seemed to enjoy. It was a steady job with a regular routine and few challenges.

Sarah apparently missed the signs that her son was developing into an attractive young man, so she was taken aback when a young lady in the church took an interest in him. Fearing that this new development could become a problem in view of Steve's poor social skills, she started to worry about how he would cope with any new relationship of a personal nature. It was time to consider what was to be done about his future.

As a Christian family, she reasoned that it was quite natural that her son might train as a minister of the church. Perhaps this was the solution. She imagined that it would be a straightforward and manageable career that would suit him well. Her limited acquaintance with the local clergy led her to suppose that, as an ordained minister, he would be able to maintain an orderly and well-regulated lifestyle. Sarah was completely unaware of the social and pastoral skills required for such a profession. The idea appealed to her; considering his shortcomings, she supposed this would protect him from any demanding 'worldly' influences.

And so, compliant as usual and with his mother's encouragement, Steve made enquiries into training for the ministry at a theological college. At her suggestion, he enrolled as a student at the Elim Bible College in London.

Once in college, free from the constraints of his mother's constant attention, Steve began to flourish. Surrounded by like-minded young students, his life became a succession of new and exciting activities. He was swept along with the crowd of students and enthusiastic probationer ministers all eager to preach the Gospel. Finally he had a new freedom that was nowhere close to the plain and simple life his mother had planned!

Back at home in Wigan, unaware of the developments at the Bible College, Sarah was gratified that she had negotiated to her satisfaction a place for her son that would ensure his moral and spiritual security. Even though he was away from home, she felt reassured that he would be safe at the Bible College and congratulated herself on what seemed to be a satisfactory arrangement. What could possibly go wrong?

To her dismay, Sarah's plans for her son's future resulted in the very thing she dreaded most. Not only had he met a student nurse in London, he brought her home for his parent's approval! Sarah was convinced that Steve was set upon a course for which he was ill-prepared. Before long, however, despite all her attempts to dissuade him and by actively discouraging the girl in question, she had to accept the fact that they had become engaged to be married.

THE LIST

As the wedding day approached, Sylvia had to confront the fact that there was a problem in her relationship with her future mother-in-law. Sarah seemed to go out of her way to be obstructive whenever they met and Sylvia was baffled by her attitude towards herself and Steve's plans to marry. As they were two mature adults with much in common, she could see no reason for Sarah's disapproval of their marriage. She hoped that Sarah would come round to accepting the situation but, as the wedding date approached, her antagonism began to make Sylvia anxious.

It was not until the day of the wedding that Sylvia realised that she had serious doubts. She felt as though she was walking through a fog. Left alone with her father at home just before leaving for the church, she sensed that something was terribly wrong. She turned to him and whispered, 'I don't want to go.'

'It's too late now,' her father replied with a smile, as he ushered her out to the waiting limousine, assuming that it was last-minute nerves but by now Sylvia was filled with alarming misgivings. Unable to summon up the courage to halt the wedding, she left the house with her father.

The ceremony felt unreal. To make matters worse, Sylvia had only met the officiating minister for the first time the night before; since they had not had a rehearsal, she discovered embarrassingly that she could not understand his strong Irish accent and she struggled to repeat the vows throughout the wedding ceremony!

After the wedding reception, Sylvia and Steve prepared to leave for their honeymoon on the south coast. As they posed for a last-minute photograph by the car, Sylvia's new mother-in-law approached her, pressed a piece of paper into her hand and whispered, 'That's his list.' Then she retreated without another word.

Rather taken aback, Sylvia pushed the note into her handbag, climbed into the car and departed with a deepening sense of unease. Later she discovered that the note contained a list of the contents of Steve's entire wardrobe – shirts, socks, underpants, and so on. She read it in disbelief, surprised both at its contents and her mother-in-law's insensitivity. It seemed so irrelevant and inappropriate on their wedding day – that day of all days! It felt bizarre but for some reason Sylvia did not mention it to her new husband and the moment passed.

In handing over that note so surreptitiously, Sarah had transferred her responsibility for her son to Sylvia as if she were handing him over to the matron of his boarding school. Unaware of what it was that Sarah was guarding so closely, Sylvia was, in all innocence, being drawn into something mysterious and unnerving. Only by degrees, and to her cost, did she discover that this was the beginning of something important, though the implications escaped her.

So far Sarah had managed to keep her fears to herself, being unwilling or unable to share them with anyone. Now the very thing she had dreaded and been trying to avoid was happening. She reluctantly acknowledged that she would have to relinquish her hold over her son; from now on, his destiny would not be in her hands. He had a wife who would eventually, and inevitably, have to bear the consequences of being married to him. Sarah would have to let him go, but she was not about to say anything and the mystery remained hidden.

FAR FROM HOME

It wasn't long before the deeper, more serious aspects of Steve and Sylvia's relationship began to emerge. After the wedding, the honeymoon ended abruptly and within the first few weeks life began to deviate from the blissful togetherness Sylvia had envisaged.

Besides her romantic expectations, her dearest wish was to be her husband's companion, partner and friend and to live out their future together in true companionship. She wanted to talk with him about their shared Christian faith, pray with him and, with all his theological training, learn from him. But it was not to be.

At first, in their new home in a lovely spacious flat in Croydon, Sylvia was impressed by Steve's easy-going manner and his willingness for her to make all the decisions. It was endearing and Sylvia enjoyed the privilege of being given a free hand. However, she soon began to find it slightly irritating that he did not seem to make any decisions.

Having put all her emotional eggs in one basket, she found it disturbing that his manner was strangely distant and that he did not seem interested in the thrill and novelty of their new married life. She lavished all her attention upon him, intent on making him happy, but her endeavours were not reciprocated. It was not long before she realised that she was in emotional limbo.

Steve seemed content to let Sylvia organise everything, just as he had always let his mother organise everything for him.He was pleasant and sociable with everyone at his church in Coulsdon but he did not develop particular relationships with any members of his congregation. At home, instead of being happy to spend time with Sylvia, he preferred to be alone or outside tinkering with the car; more often than not he would sit in front of the television without showing any real interest in the programme. Sylvia was frequently frustrated that he did not show any interest in current affairs, books, newspapers or conversation.

Given the choice, he rarely deviated from routine and disliked change; he was quite happy letting his increasingly frustrated wife arrange everything. Sylvia hardly dared entertain the awful thought that she was married to a stranger! It was as if she were seeing him for the first time.

In his capacity as the church minister, Steve preached interesting sermons on Sundays that were well received by the members of the congregation. They were not aware that his messages had been copied in longhand on Saturday nights while he watched the television.

Being far from home, and in the absence of her girlfriends to talk to, Sylvia fell into the habit of keeping her uneasy thoughts to herself. Within a few weeks of being married, she became isolated and lonely. In her new job at the local health centre in Croydon, her primary social contacts were her health visitor colleagues and occasionally some of the ladies from church. The rest of the time she and Steve were alone with not much to talk about!

Steve's mother frequently came to stay with them as if she needed to continue overseeing her son's affairs. She baked, cleaned, shopped and generally made herself useful about their home. This amount of attention was unwelcome as far as Sylvia was concerned. She felt as if she were under constant surveillance. Was she fulfilling her role as her son's wife to her mother-in-law's satisfaction?

It created an uncomfortable amount of tension between them but her unconcerned husband saw nothing amiss in his mother's frequent visits or the way she took control when she visited them. He was entirely oblivious to Sylvia's discomfort. After all, this was what he was used to; it was familiar and comforting with his mother in charge. It seemed that it was a case of 'mother knows best', even though he was married.

They were still living in the flat in Croydon two years after their marriage when they broke the news that Sylvia was pregnant with their first child. Sarah was visibly shaken – it was as though they had given her news of a death instead of a birth. When Sylvia enquired about her reaction, she replied that she was concerned about how they would manage. Sylvia supposed that she meant how would they manage in a situation over which her mother-in-law had no control!

With Sarah's overbearing influence even when she was not physically with them, and Steve's reluctance to engage in the preparations for the forthcoming baby, Sylvia became increasingly anxious and the pregnancy did not go well. In the absence of any emotional or physical support, Sylvia's usual self-confidence evaporated, especially as Steve showed no interest or excitement at the prospect of becoming a parent. She was pregnant in London without her friends and away from all that was familiar.

It may have been due to the increased stress that she developed the debilitating condition in pregnancy known as hyperemesis, marked by severe nausea that persisted throughout the day and night. She lost weight and, with the resulting weakness, had to be admitted to hospital where she felt even more isolated as Steve's lack of concern became increasingly apparent

When she was discharged from the hospital, Sylvia's nausea continued and she needed Steve's presence and support even more. His response was to take a part-time job as a coach driver with a local company driving the guards at Buckingham Palace on and off duty. Together with his church commitments, this resulted in long hours away from home, leaving Sylvia alone. Once again her mother-in-law came to stay, and this time Sylvia was glad of her company. Being far from home without the support of her own mother and family and friends, she was in desperate need of care and attention.

When the baby was born, they named her Susan. Sylvia expected her husband to share in her pride and joy, and longed for his emotional support and practical help, but welcoming their baby together was not to be. He seemed to be unaware that he had a role to play, nor did he notice Sylvia's vulnerability as a new mother in a strange place.

She had given up her full-time job as a health visitor. During the time she was working, she had not had the opportunity to meet their neighbours; most of whom were away during the day, travelling into the city each morning to work. Most of the time the area around the flat was deserted and Sylvia had the lovely, peaceful neighbourhood all to herself. But it was a lonely place and, with only her baby for company, she felt isolated and depressed.

Her health visitor, a former colleague, responded to Sylvia's emotional and social needs by matching her up with another lonely mother, a diplomat's wife, who unfortunately left with her husband for another posting soon after they became acquainted.

Soon after Susan's first birthday, Steve was relocated by the Bible College to pastor a small Elim Church in Dudley in the Midlands. Sylvia was happier there as she was finally able to meet other young mums and make friends. However, entertaining their new friends in their home soon proved to be a problem. Steve, although amiable and superficially friendly, developed the habit of leaving the room without warning when he had had enough of their company, leaving Sylvia to carry on entertaining their guests by herself. She found this bizarre behaviour difficult and embarrassing but out of necessity she became adept at covering up for him and making excuses. In time, their friends stopped visiting.

Covering up for Steve's problematic behaviour, Sylvia felt as though she was turning into a replica of his mother and, like his mother, she could not discuss her worries with anyone. As a nurse, she had tried many times to find an answer to the elusive symptoms of his problem but, as she had no experience and limited access to relevant information about behavioural issues, she drew a blank. She was tenaciously loyal, reluctant to discuss the frustrating situation or Steve's conduct with anyone, knowing that it would certainly damage his reputation and his ministry. What could she say? His odd behaviour went unsuspected by casual acquaintances and his insensitivity and lack of empathy were not detected by those who had only superficial contact with him.

Time and time again she reflected on how they had appeared to get along so well before they were married. She continually asked herself how she could have been so unaware of the problem. Admittedly they were never alone for long periods during their courtship days and hardly ever discussed serious matters, but somehow she had dismissed the significance of their superficial relationship.

Had she read too much into their friendship, overlooking the fact that they had very few interests in common? Had she been too ready to go along with his schoolboy humour that always seemed to deflect them from serious conversations? Or was the problem rooted in the over-protective and all-encompassing influence of his mother, who also manipulated difficult situations so effectively and disguised Steve's inability to make decisions for himself? All the same she felt cheated. Even now, his mother was still covering up her son's immature behaviour. Sylvia was resentful of her mother-in-law's involvement in their marriage and her interference in every aspect of their lives.

Their complicated and frustrating lifestyle in Dudley continued until their daughter's second birthday when Sarah made one of her frequent visits. As usual she busied herself about the house for a few days until she was satisfied that everything was in order, then prepared to return home. The day she left they waved her goodbye, not knowing it was the last time they would see her alive. Sarah returned home and died in her sleep that night.

Her fears and concerns about her son, so well hidden over the years, died with her but their destructive influence was silently and insidiously transferred to Sylvia. It affected every part of their lives. Sarah had not so much as hinted that there was a problem in all the years that Sylvia had known her; when she died, she left Sylvia to bear the consequences and incur a great deal of hurt and unhappiness along the way.

Although she grieved for her mother-in-law with the rest of the family, Sylvia felt betrayed by her unbending attitude over the years. It was as if Sarah had been blocking her out from something she had every right to know. The fact was that, for some unknown reason, Steve had relied on his mother even after their marriage. Now Sylvia was left to deal with his problem, whatever it was, alone.

In despair, she realized she was married to a man who was incapable of coping with life's challenges in general and the responsibilities of being a husband and father in particular. She thought she had married someone strong and capable, for that was the impression he had given when they first met. But that was far from the truth and now, with Sarah gone, Sylvia felt the weight of responsibility for him and their child even more.

She was confused and did not know where to turn or what to do. She prayed, but the heavens were silent. 'Where is God in all this?' she cried. She felt cheated; Why was He not answering her prayers, and why was He not there when they needed Him? She was facing the prospect of the future alone and with dread.

ORDINATION - A SECOND CHANCE

Steve struggled to cope after his mother's death. Eventually, when he completed his time as a probationer, his ordination was deferred. His inability to fulfil his pastoral duties satisfactorily had become apparent and his future as an Elim minister was not to be realized.

Disappointed, Steve left the Elim Church and for a while he was unemployed. However, after a short time at the age of thirty, he was able to secure a place in the West Midlands Police Force but, under the circumstances, he and Sylvia found it difficult to settle in Dudley and eventually they decided to move away.

Steve transferred to a new police authority and they bought a house in a quiet village on the outskirts of town north of Dudley. They began to settle down and, in due course, their second daughter was born and at last hey began to make friends.

The local Anglican minister welcomed them as new members of his congregation, and becoming part of the friendly church had a beneficial effect upon the whole family. Upon learning of Steve's theological training, and seeing him as a potential candidate for the Anglican ministry, he suggested that he might consider ordination. So it was that, with the encouragement and guidance of Peter, the vicar, Steve began training part time for the Anglican ministry alongside his full-time position as a police officer. He was eventually ordained as a non-stipendiary priest at Lichfield Cathedral. The promises he made at his ordination raised Sylvia's hopes. Perhaps everything was going to be all right after all.

Sylvia was grateful for Peter and his wife's genuine friendship; meeting them had an invaluable effect upon Steve, which in turn improved their family life immensely. Peter assumed the role of mentor to Steve, sharing with him his expertise and wisdom; it was as if he intuitively discerned Steve's inadequacy and respected his limitations.

As a part-time, non-stipendiary minister, Steve was not required to fulfil the responsibilities of a full-time minister but assisted at the Sunday services when he was available. For a while life settled into a comparatively quiet domestic routine, as long as Sylvia held the reins and took responsibility for the smooth running of all their affairs and Steve had the positive motivation and support provided by their friend Peter and his family.

Sylvia and Steve's new life in the village environment brought about a more relaxed atmosphere in their home. Caring for the baby and Susan, their nine-year-old daughter, helped Sylvia attain a certain measure of peace, filling her emotional vacuum with love and companionship, thankful too, that with the friendship and support of their new friends in the local church, she began to hope for a more harmonious lifestyle. However, the atmosphere in their home was not entirely peaceful as Steve was still unable to contribute or engage consistently in the life and happiness of his family.

Looking back, it is not difficult to see why they limped from crisis to crisis in their relationship,for there was indeed a tremendous schism over which they had no understanding or control, affecting every aspect of their lives. Without expert intervention of any sort they were floundering, tragically unaware of the magnitude of the situation in which they were engulfed. The dark shadow of the unknown remained a constant threat to their marriage as they struggled to deal with the hidden challenges stacked up against them.

Frequently perplexed and constantly frustrated, Sylvia found comfort and support in the friends she had made in the village, although she was unable to share her most troubled thoughts with them. Prayer helped and eventually she became resigned to the situation and stopped asking 'Why?'.

acknowledging that there was something missing but she did not know what! It was a case of self preservation that led her to acknowledging the emotional stalemate. Sometimes, with rare flashes of insight, she caught a glimpse of Steve's perplexing situation too. But that was unknown territory and she shied away from it, concentrating all her efforts into trying to create a happy family life.

PEACE UNDER PRESSURE

As the years rolled by with a constant undercurrent of anxiety, Sylvia tried to hold her peace for the sake of her children and husband. But, with the passage of time, it became increasingly difficult. There was still no one she felt able to confide in, even though she was tempted on numerous occasions.

The friends they had made over the years accepted them without knowing about the secret but Sylvia hated the fact that it was always there, overshadowing their friendships. It was the penalty she was forced to pay to preserve her husband's reputation and good standing in the community and the church. Although he cooperated when encouraged to join the social life of the village, the atmosphere at home behind closed doors remained strained.

Sylvia yearned for the close companionship of like minds, the support of a loving husband and a normal family life. Instead it was hard work coaxing Steve out of his isolation. She struggled constantly to suppress the bitterness and resentment that was robbing her of a peaceful and happy marriage but despite the lack of any prospect of change and ever the optimist, she was hopeful that one day things would improve.

Sadly, on the contrary, as time passed Steve became increasingly isolated and distant and Sylvia became correspondingly more anxious and frustrated. Try as she might, she could not rid herself of the notion that any sign of a mental problem was something not to be discussed but rather to be hidden. She was afraid of the stigma attached to it, unable to voice her fears; she was suffering in silence because of the shame.

FUN, FELLOWSHIP AND FOOD

On the brighter side, as an active member of the local church Sylvia became the leader of a youth fellowship that began as a confirmation class but developed into what they called the 'Friday Night Fun, Fellowship and Food Night'. The fellowship was great and the Bible teaching meaningful, but Sylvia suspected that the food was the draw!

It was a place where the children, mostly pre-teens, were free to express themselves without being judged. The class grew so big that the dividing wall in Steve and Sylvia's living room was knocked down to accommodate them all. Eventually, because of the growing numbers, a young man from the church joined the group to help. When the six-week confirmation class ended, the Friday night meetings continued for more than two years and became a focal point for the young people of the village as they matured into happy, well-adjusted young people.

Sometimes Steve came home from work in his police uniform during the Friday night meetings. The overawed children immediately quietened down, expecting him to stop and talk with them. Even though it was obvious that the children would have loved him to join them, and would have willingly hung on his every word, Steve would pass through the eager group with a brief hello and vanish into the kitchen or the bedroom until they left. How Sylvia berated him – what a lost opportunity to talk to those impressionable youngsters! Her frustration frequently turned to anger but nothing moved him. He never changed and nothing was gained.

About that time just as they seemed to have reached a comparatively settled life in the village, there was a significant change affecting all their lives. Peter, their friend and vicar, was transferred to a benefice in Lancashire. Steve felt the loss of Peter's support and friendship keenly; it was the only close relationship he had known and once again he struggled to deal with a change of circumstances. Sylvia also missed Peter's steadying influence on Steve, who had been Peters protégé to a great extent. His wise mentoring had frequently guided Steve through challenging situations that he would have found insurmountable alone

Without Peter's advice and support, Steve's social life and general conduct took a downward turn. Despite Sylvia's best efforts, their family life reverted to tension and discord. Whenever their father returned home, the children sensed a change in the atmosphere and they often disappeared to occupy themselves elsewhere. The girls loved their father but he rarely showed any enthusiasm for anything that interested them. Sylvia would distract their attention and, as they grew up, they simply accepted that was how things were.

Sometimes when they were alone, desperate to talk and pick up where Peter had left off, Sylvia would try to draw Steve into quiet conversation and show him that he was loved. He resisted any such advances and shied away from intimate discussions. Pleading with him to open up to her, Sylvia would remind him that she was his wife, not his mother and that she loved him. He responded by withdrawing further into an impenetrable silence, as though she were scolding him. Even after years of marriage, he had a mindset that Sylvia could not understand; if he was frustrated, she was even more so.

Their life together was neither rewarding nor fulfilling, belying their Christian reputation. Sylvia found the contrast between their public and private lives deeply disturbing and, inevitably, it drove them further apart. On reflection, she knew that on many occasions she did not handle the situation well but she did not know what to do and was often at her wits' end. The happiness she craved eluded her.

LEAVING THE NEST

At the age of seventeen, their elder daughter, Susan, left home for the first time to begin her ophthalmic nurse training. At this turning point in her life, she could see more clearly how the dynamics of their family functioned.

Sylvia had shielded the girls from much of the friction when they were growing up; even now, Susan only saw her father as amiable, passive and compliant, and Sylvia as the domineering parent who did all the organising and who set the standards of discipline in the home often making her unpopular. Steve never admonished or disciplined Susan or her sister. In Sylvia's defence, she had always encouraged the girls to respect their father, giving him his rightful place at home and deferring to him in all important matters. The girls loved him and did not hold his shortcomings against him.

Now that Susan was ready to fly the nest she had her own agenda. Her life was full of all the things that occupy young people; she looked forward to fulfilling her own destiny – and that included falling in love!

She met her future husband while she was a student nurse during her training. Before long, they became engaged and planned to marry as soon as she had completed her final examinations.

At the engagement party, Sylvia once again found herself covering up for Steve, fearing that Susan's prospective in-laws might notice his difficulty in coping with the social challenges the occasion presented. She did not want them to consider him insensitive or wonder where he was when he escaped to another room to avoid them during the festivities. The newly-engaged couple were happy, surrounded by love and good wishes. It was a day of celebration and Sylvia intended things to stay that way for as long as possible.

Her daughter's joy accentuated Sylvia's unhappiness. The engagement was the beginning of Sylvia's descent into dark despair. Despite all the years of attempting to keep the tormenting secret at bay by maintaining a semblance of normality, Sylvia's mental and emotional composure began to crumble.

Notwithstanding the stresses at home, Sylvia's professional life as a health visitor was satisfying and fulfilling. She worked mostly with parents and young families in their homes and in clinics and schools. She often had a significant role in court proceedings regarding serious child-protection issues. Being trained to deal with difficult situations and appreciated for her expertise in the responsible role she held at work gave her a sense of worth. However, while supporting her daughter during her final nursing examinations and preparing for her wedding, Sylvia's life became increasingly stressful. A dark cloud was threatening the happiness surrounding the forthcoming marriage.

THE DECISION

Until then, Sylvia had managed to keep the mounting pressure in check but with Susan's engagement their circumstances began to change. The thought of living without her daughter's supporting presence at home once she was married filled Sylvia with dread. She realized that it was because of Susan, and the love and companionship she and sister provided, that she had been able to tolerate the unrelenting frustration and loneliness for so long. Now her life as she had known it was teetering on the edge of collapse and she felt as though she was losing control. It was at that point that she made up her mind; the only course of action was to leave, to run away, to escape.

Planning to leave just before her daughter's wedding was certainly not the best time to make such a drastic decision but the prospect of Susan leaving home was the catalyst; the decision was made. Once Susan left home, Sylvia would leave too.

She made a last-ditch attempt to discuss the reason she was leaving with Steve, hoping for some sort of breakthrough, but he was unreachable and whatever she said made no sense to him. As in the past, his reaction to face-to-face confrontation was to become angry and walk away, refusing to discuss the problem.

Even then, although frustrated and desperate, Sylvia still hoped for a miraculous turn around. She did not give credence to the awful thoughts that crowded her mind, thoughts that were telling her that there was a problem with her husband's ability to comprehend the dire situation. Had his capacity to understand deteriorated to such a degree that he was beyond understanding? Why would he not talk to her and say how he felt?

They were going round and round in circles and getting nowhere. At the time, Sylvia neither knew nor understood that there was a reason; she only knew that she was caught in a downward spiral of despair.

A CHILL WIND BLOWS

Having finally decided to leave, Sylvia made arrangements to move into her own home. By the time of the wedding several weeks later, she had moved to a house across town, taking their younger daughter Jane with her.

When the news of their separation became known in the village, Steve naturally had the support of the local church. The members were mystified as to why Sylvia had left him and he could not give them an answer. The church members perceived his bewilderment as sadness and regret, emotions that were unfamiliar to him. Without the benefit of facts, they speculated why Sylvia would do such a thing and proceeded to vilify her. Friends, family, colleagues and acquaintances indulged in all kinds of speculation.

People Sylvia had known for years turned away from her and some of her colleagues avoided her. Of course, they had no idea about the lengths to which she had resorted to preserve their marriage – the prayers in the night, the tears, the constant questioning and self-blame accompanying the guilt and confusion.

She had tried to persuade Steve to seek help several times in the past to no avail. 'What help?' he would ask. He did not see the need. On one occasion even their general practitioner, seeing how stressed Sylvia was, tried to help by referring them to a marriage guidance counsellor as a matter of urgency. Steve reluctantly agreed to attend but the appointment with the counsellor came to an abrupt end when Steve's attitude became hostile and aggressive. The session ended inconclusively; they left with an invitation from the counsellor to return at a later date but that never happened.

Various Christian and non-Christian individuals tried to help but Steve managed to evade the issue each time and numerous arrangements fell through. On one occasion they travelled to

Yorkshire to the home of a fellow Pentecostal friend and spent an entire day receiving counselling and prayers – but they left without a breakthrough. As they said their good-byes, Steve's friends were in tears. Sylvia was beyond tears and yet Steve was apparently unmoved. It became obvious that there was no one who could give the answer they needed.

Regarding the separation, the general public were denied an explanation from Sylvia. The pain of twenty-five years could not be explained in a sentence and she did not have an easy answer to give. She had no intention of satisfying their idle curiosity anyway! Most of them assumed she had left her husband for another man; when that theory did not stand up to scrutiny, they looked for other reasons to judge her.

Sylvia kept the reason why she left to herself and consequently incurred the most excoriating criticism from the local Christian community. It was only then that she realised how few Christian friends she had, and how quickly the friends she thought she had backed off! Of course, it was partly because she had distanced herself from them by leaving the village, but no-one followed her to find out what the problem was or to offer their support. The tide of opinion flowed in Steve's direction, testament to how well-known and popular he was in the church. How could Sylvia counteract that without tarnishing his reputation?

It was an unreal situation. Naturally people compared Sylvia to him; after all, he was the one they saw regularly in the pulpit and shaking their hands at the church door. It was hard for Sylvia to bear.

Initially it was non-Christians, people she hardly knew, who befriended her. People from the weirdest religious sects – and sometimes none – offered their friendship and sincerely tried to help, surprising her with their compassion. One individual even advocated hypnotism, suggesting that it might alleviate the problem (whatever that problem was!).

Ironically, it was a stranger, a non-Christian,who seemed to understand. Upon hearing that Sylvia had left her husband for no apparent reason, this person intuitively observed that it must have been something really serious for her to prefer to live alone rather than remain married to Steve. That was indeed the truth but not many of the people who knew her best were willing to give her the benefit of the doubt, least of all the people she had thought were her friends.

FOR BETTER OR FOR WORSE

As with the engagement party, their daughter's wedding was traumatic. Sylvia realized too late that she had misjudged the impact of leaving just before such an important occasion. She had been so desperate to leave that she'd convinced herself that it did not make any difference to the occasion. Perhaps no one would be interested.

Despite everything, the day passed well for everyone apart from Steve and Sylvia. As the parents of the bride, they struggled to play their part. Sylvia stayed out of Steve's way for most of the time. He was on his own from now on, she reasoned. She had given up covering for him once and for all; nevertheless, she felt wretched and anxious. The habits of a lifetime were not easy to break.

Witnessing the young couple making their vows accentuated Steve and Sylvia's situation. It reminded Sylvia of the vows they had made on their wedding day when, even with her doubts, she had hoped for the best without any intention of breaking her vows. She had believed optimistically that everything would turn out just as she desired. As a committed Christian she never thought she would ever consider divorce.

The realization of what she had done was devastating. She was heartbroken; it was not at all what she had planned and her dream had turned into a nightmare. The signs had been obvious right from the start but, like many a bride, she thought she could change Steve!

The phrase 'for better or for worse' was what they had promised; she had held on to the prospect of things changing for the better when, in fact, they had turned out to be far worse than she could possibly have imagined.

Having that terrible responsibility dumped on her as a young and innocent bride had felt like a curse and she had lived under its shadow for all those years without respite. But, as bad as things were, she might have coped because she loved him if only her mother-in-law had confided in her, or even hinted that there was a problem and been more open with her support.

Sarah could have helped Sylvia to understand Steve more but that was not in her nature. She was not particularly easy to talk to at the best of times, so it was unlikely she would have been inclined to talk about something so difficult and confusing. Perhaps she had a problem, too.

It was not rebellion but a weariness of the soul that motivated Sylvia to leave. As far as she could see, she was staring defeat in the face and she was no longer willing to go on with the curse hanging over her head. But within days of making the drastic decision, she was tormented by the enormity of the situation and could not bring herself to finally let go. She weighed the gravity of the situation once again, full of remorse and deeply distressed.

She felt the need to talk to Steve urgently at least once more. Surely there was some vestige of their ruined marriage that could be salvaged? She was aware that she was back-tracking but she had to accept that it was too late. There was no use trying to retrieve the disastrous marriage now; the vacuum had already been filled. An eligible lady, a divorcee with a young child and a member of the church, was already waiting in the wings ready to take her place. Within a few days she had stepped into Sylvia's shoes.

A CASE OF NO RETURN

The circumstances were such that there was no going back. Sylvia felt as though the world was falling apart around her and the devil was dancing with glee. Another born-again Christian bites the dust!

Days passed; resigned to the hopeless situation, Sylvia expected some relief but there was none. She felt agitated and unsettled. She had got what she wanted but it brought no peace.

Steve, however, apparently behaved almost as if nothing of importance had happened. He had welcomed another woman into his life willingly and the gap had closed seamlessly. He was cosseted and surrounded by sympathy and devoted attention. There were people around him bolstering his ego, making light of his responsibilities, making life easy for him with their constant attention. The general opinion in the church and the wider community who knew him only as an ordained priest was that he had been treated badly. Sylvia was the one who had destroyed the marriage; he was the innocent party.

She was ostracised and made to feel unwelcome. Even some close members of her own family judged her; she was condemned to pay the price for her presumed wickedness. She had kept the secret so well that no one suspected the emotional and mental anguish she had suffered over the years. They had no inkling of the stress that had eventually tipped her over the edge. How trivial they would consider the arguments in her defence if she were to try to justify her actions. This man, the supposed injured party, was, to all who knew him outside the confines of their home, above reproach, even when he moved in with the new woman with no pangs of conscience while still being married to Sylvia.

Initially there was no contact from Steve, as if after twenty-five years the marriage had never been – a case of 'out of sight, out of mind'. He was content to follow someone else's wishes, obligingly accepting the suggestion of a divorce. He turned up at Sylvia's home one day and requested a divorce as though he had been sent on an errand. For her it felt like the end of her life; she was devastated, even though that life had at times been one of abject misery.

A FRIEND IN NEED

In the midst of all the approbation surrounding Steve, one voice from an unexpected quarter challenged the general opinion that he was innocent and entirely blameless.

A churchwarden, a close associate of Steve's in one of the sister churches and a man Sylvia would have described only as an acquaintance, stood out from the flow of goodwill their priest was enjoying and spoke out in her defence. Over the years, he had been associated with Steve in relation to the services and the general management of church affairs. Sylvia knew him to be a man of integrity, dedicated to his responsibilities. Unlike the assembly surrounding Steve, he had recognized a series of inconsistencies in his fellow churchman's behaviour that were concealed by the smokescreen of popularity.

When the news broke that Sylvia had left Steve, he alone was not surprised. He had had serious doubts about the situation. As a churchwarden and an official of the church, he had exercised discretion over what he had observed in the past but, in view of the present circumstances, he decided to speak out about his concerns and let it be known that, in his opinion, Sylvia was being misjudged. The scandal circulated around the village and the gossips had a field day. The warden, however, felt the bad publicity keenly and was greatly distressed, not only for Sylvia but for the church as well.

Apart from his lone voice, Sylvia felt a complete lack of support. She decided to move away from the village church that had been her spiritual home for nearly fourteen years but had now become a 'no-go area'. She visited a church within travelling distance of her new home but, since the news of her leaving her husband followed her, she was greeted cautiously. Feeling uncomfortable, Sylvia withdrew; she was not accustomed to being considered the subject of suspicion.

She was in spiritual limbo, without Christian friends or fellowship, and the chill wind of loneliness and despair started to creep into her soul.

THE BOUGH BREAKS

It was New Year's Eve. It had been a long day and, as the evening approached, Sylvia felt depression closing in around her. She was alone on the eve of a new year, with neither friends or family close by. She had no one to share it with and no one to talk to or confide in. She missed Susan her newly married daughter so much. As if to emphasize her loneliness, a party was in progress next door. She could hear their merry-making and laughter spilling out into the night. The loud music and dancing echoed out across the street in anticipation of the New Year.

Sylvia wasn't conscious of feeling suicidal; she was too confused to think of anything so specific. She just felt desperately lonely and depressed. She wanted everything to stop. She could see no logic in the way her life was turning out. Thoughts of failure spun around in her head, dragging her downwards. She moved about the house restlessly and aimlessly on auto-pilot. Her younger daughter, Jane, had left earlier in the evening to spend time with her friend, leaving Sylvia alone at home.

As she wandered about the house, her mind drifted back to her past in Salford. She thought of the reassuring presence of her Auntie Ada in the years of her childhood and how she had missed her when she and Steve married and moved away to live in Surrey. Her aunt and both of her parents were long dead, and her brothers and sister no longer featured in her life; she had lost contact with all but one of her siblings All had gone their separate ways. They had never had anything in common apart from their unhappy childhood.

Waves of nausea swept over her. She felt disorientated and exhausted beyond anything she had ever felt before. She wanted to cry but there was no relief and the tears would not come. After a while, she sat at the dining table and started to write. Writing came easily to her, she would normally make notes and lists as a matter of course, so writing in this instance was an automatic response, an outlet for her distressing train of thoughts.

She wrote as though the act of putting her distorted thoughts down on paper would clear the confusion but it was impossible to release pain onto paper. She was in a state of indescribable grief, trying to express the inexpressible, her thoughts alternating between one despairing notion and another. She longed to escape the tumult raging inside her head.

She was offloading her deepest thoughts about her desire to be free of the burden of living the nightmare her life had become. Expressing her thoughts about who would look after Jane if she was not there, she was writing as if she were having a discussion with herself without coming to any conclusion. Thoughts and words flowed unchecked, regardless of the wisdom of speculating about ending her life.

In the end she could not even consider leaving Jane with her irresponsible father and the conversation with herself about "ending it all" was inconclusive because it meant she would have to leave Jane behind, but in writing down such confused thoughts about Jane, she had left herself wide open to the incriminating consequences that might follow any suggestion of taking Jane with her. Just writing it down was an expression of how disorientated she was. In that state, there was no way she could have explained her complex train of thoughts to anyone, nor could she explain the need to write the letters.

Her mind still in a fog, she addressed a letter to Steve, telling him of her deep heartache, sorrow, and pain. This was followed by several letters to her friends and family; she wrote until she had exhausted her troubled thoughts.

Taking the letters out to the car, she drove to the home of the churchwarden and his wife, the only people she thought would understand her state of mind. She posted the bundle through the letterbox of their home with a note asking them, irrationally, not to open it until tomorrow.

As she returned home, a faint spark of hope flickered through her mind. Would they see this as a cry for help and come to her aid?

As she had predicted, the warden's wife telephoned her within minutes of her return, greatly concerned about the letters. She tried to comfort Sylvia but, finding her so upset, she announced that they were coming to her straight away.

Listening to her reassuring voice, Sylvia instantly felt a sense of relief. Help was on the way. But they did not come as they had said they would and what followed that fateful night was a travesty of the truth!

As Sylvia waited for her friends, Jane returned home. Not wishing her daughter to witness her distress, Sylvia ushered Jane upstairs to her bedroom. She took a glass of cherryade and a snack to her room with her.

On an impulse, Sylvia gave Jane half of one of her sleeping tablets, hoping it would settle her. Her nursing experience assured her that half a sleeping tablet would be safe to give to a healthy young girl who was above average height for her age.

With her daughter safely upstairs preparing for bed, Sylvia returned to the sitting room to await her friends' arrival. By now she was beginning to feel the effects of overwhelming mental and emotional fatigue, reinforced by an unaccustomed glass of sherry because, she remembered, they always had sherry on New Year's Eve!

In the living room, as she sat in the chair beside her desk, she began to feel drowsy. Closing her eyes, she started to relax a little, still holding the glass of sherry in her hand.

HAPPY NEW YEAR

Suddenly the front door burst open and the room was invaded by a blast of cold air and a terrifying number of uniformed policemen, accompanied by a doctor. They found Sylvia sitting in her armchair holding a glass of sherry. Jane was upstairs watching television.

'What have you done?' shouted the officer in charge, rushing towards Sylvia.

She froze in fear and alarm as the police ran into the room and into the kitchen, ransacking the cupboards and looking for evidence. Shocked and shaken by the sudden frenzy of activity erupting around her, Sylvia was unable to take in the enormity of the situation. She was no match for the aggressive police officers crowding into her home firing accusations at her.

The kitchen cupboard revealed a packet of paracetamol tablets; upstairs in her bedside drawer they found her sleeping tablets and they triumphantly retrieved the bottle of sherry from the dining-room table. As they were confiscating these items, Sylvia heard a police officer in the kitchen speak into his mobile radio. 'She has been plying the child with sleeping tablets and sherry,' he lied.

They were joined by her next-door neighbour. The man was helping them gleefully, suggesting places to look and enjoying the unexpected excitement. Sylvia remained seated, dumb with shock and unable to move.

The doctor, summoned by Sylvia's friends, pushed forward. With his hands in his greatcoat pockets, he swaggered into view and stood over her. She looked up at him and saw nothing but disdain in his expression. 'What have you given your daughter?' he demanded repeatedly.

There was no compassion in his voice or his attitude. Hostility emanated from his very being, oozing through his expensive winter coat. He did not see a fellow human being, a potential patient crushed and in desperate need of his professional help. The individual before him was obviously a criminal!

Standing at a distance in front of Sylvia, he apparently detected no medical sign worthy of his attention. Observing nothing that assisted him in making a diagnosis, he turned away impatiently from the distraught woman before him with no hint of professional integrity and muttered something to the officer in charge.

As he turned to leave, the doctor stepped into the hallway and came face to face with the subject of his emergency call. Jane, the child allegedly at risk who was supposedly in imminent danger, was standing halfway up the stairs. Stopping momentarily and throwing a glance in her direction, he callously announced, 'Don't you know that your mother just tried to kill you?' Then he turned towards the front door where he made his exit, leaving the frightened child standing transfixed in terror on the stairs.

At this point, Sylvia's would-be rescuers, the churchwarden and his wife, arrived amid the chaos and were horrified at the scene before them. They rushed to her side with cries of alarm, not realising that the information they had given the doctor over the telephone out of their fear for Sylvia's safety had been translated by him into a major criminal incident. They had arrived expecting to find him calmly attending Sylvia, evaluating her mental and emotional distress. Instead they witnessed his departure shocked at his dismissive attitude, the whole frenzied scene exacerbating Sylvia's already distraught state of mind.

It was evident that his brief visit that night had been an inconvenient call-out during his New Year celebrations. His response, based on the briefest information, had been to summon the police before even assessing the situation. By involving the police, his unprofessional action precipitated the ensuing disastrous outcome.

Upon arrival, the police dealt with the situation as a scene of a crime. After a short, unproductive interview with Sylvia, who was undeniably in a state of shock, they cautioned and arrested her for administering a noxious substance to a juvenile.

At this point, apart from the incredibly unbelievable self-incriminating letters written by the woman in front of them who was passive to the point of inertia and demonstrating no obvious signs of having carried out a criminal act, there was no actual evidence of her having administered any noxious substance to her daughter. Nor had they or the doctor made any attempt to interview or examine the juvenile in question.

Bewildered and trembling uncontrollably, Sylvia was escorted to the waiting police car with its flashing lights. It was surrounded by New Year party revellers. Vaguely, as if in a trance, Sylvia was aware that the street was packed with her neighbours and curious onlookers and the street parties had come to a temporary standstill.

The church bells rang out the new year as she climbed into the police car and sitting beside her a female police officer wished everyone 'Happy New Year!'.

At the police station, Sylvia was photographed at the regulation angles and finger printed and before she was locked in a cell she was relieved of her bra! Although the police officers in charge of her arrest were cold and indifferent, the young officer recording her personal effects looked at Sylvia with an expression that conveyed his discomfort at her treatment by his colleagues. It was as though he was thinking of his mother, who was of a similar age to Sylvia, and how he would feel had she been treated in such a manner. That was the only fleeting glimpse of compassion Sylvia, confused and embarrassed, experienced that night.

The officers unceremoniously locked her in a cell where she stood, gazing numb and unbelieving at the blank tiled walls, the bench secured to the floor and the toilet in the corner. She felt abandoned, helpless and afraid.

She was left for what seemed like several hours while the arresting officers completed their paperwork at leisure. They had apparently tried to contact Steve but, since he had moved into his lady friend's home, they were unable to reach him. This was, of course, before the days of mobile phones.

Eventually a solicitor on call was contacted but, because he was at a New Year party and had been drinking alcohol, he could not attend that night. He agreed to come the following morning. There was nothing else to be done by the police on duty that night. All the boxes had been ticked. Job done!

THE PREMONITION

Alone in the dimly-lit cell, Sylvia's mind and emotions were in meltdown. She called out for help several times but her cries were ignored. The night dragged on as, helpless and uncomprehending, she tried to make sense of the mayhem surrounding her.

After a while, at some point during the night, her mind cleared. She remembered an extraordinary incident that had occurred the previous day at home. She had been resting with her eyes closed in the armchair beside her desk when a vision of disaster striking the house had flashed before her. In the vision, there was a mighty explosion above her, bringing the ceiling and walls crashing down on to the furniture and everything in the room. Dust rose from the force of the impact and debris fell all around her. All the furniture in the room was reduced to rubble except for the armchair. Sylvia was unharmed and the chair remained intact, without a single scratch. Then, in an instant, the dramatic scene disappeared and she had opened her eyes to realise that it had not actually happened. But such was the power and intensity of the vision that she was left shaken and afraid.

She had had no idea what it could possibly be and concluded that perhaps it was a forewarning of a problem with the gas boiler or some such thing. When nothing happened over the next few hours, she had pushed the thoughts of an imminent disaster to the back of her mind and tried to forget the incident. But it had left her feeling uneasy, anticipating a more sinister outcome than the gas boiler exploding.

Confined in the police cell, Sylvia recalled the premonition and wondered if it had been a warning about the situation she was in now. On reflection, she realised that only a few hours ago she had been sitting in her armchair when the police stormed in, bringing her world crashing down around her. She recognized, too, that the premonition had not only been a warning but also a message of preservation and reassurance.

Faint and exhausted, Sylvia lay on the hard bench, refusing to touch the grubby-looking blanket. She wrapped her coat around her and shivered throughout the long night, not sure whether through nerves or the cold – probably both! She continually turned over in her mind the significance of the premonition then, in the silence, she remembered some words from the Bible: 'In God I have put my trust, I will not be afraid. What can man do to me?'

Strangely, her spirits lifted as she waited for the morning. Her predominant thoughts, however, were for her daughter and what had happened to her.

NEW YEAR'S EVE

JANE'S ACCOUNT (Aged 13 years)

I was watching a special *EastEnders*' New Year's Eve programme on the television in my room. I had taken a glass of cherryade and some shortbread to my room.

Mum seemed a bit upset. Maybe she thought I might get upset too, so she gave me half of one of her sleeping tablets to help me sleep because things were not very happy for us at that time. Mum sometimes took a sleeping tablet to help her sleep, and she was probably trying to make things easier for me that night. The next thing I knew was a lot of noise downstairs.

When I saw the police, I thought they had come for me! I was really scared because Mum did not know that my friend and I had been down to the pub on the estate earlier that night. I thought I was in trouble. We had only looked in; we knew we couldn't have a drink but we were curious. I thought the police had come for me but instead they were shouting at Mum.

I was frightened by the things they were saying to her, although I couldn't understand what it was all about. When the policeman saw me, he asked, 'What has your mother given you?' It made no sense to me and I just stood in one spot while they rushed about the house and questioned Mum.

When I started to come down the stairs, a man who must have been a doctor looked up at me and said, 'Don't you know your mother just tried to kill you?' Then he left. I stood on the staircase for a long time then I went back upstairs feeling very worried.

Soon they all left and took Mum away with them. The house was empty and I did not know what to do, so I went out for a walk through the streets. When I got back, our next-door neighbour came around and spoke to me. She asked me to go round to her house for the rest of the night and let me sleep in one of their beds.

I think she got in touch with the police the next morning to ask them who was going to look after me but no one seemed to know. I don't think anyone cared about me.

I stayed next door for the next three days before Dad came to pick me up. He took me to stay with him and a lady I had never met. I think she was from his church. I wanted to be with Mum, but they wouldn't let me see her.

REMANDED IN CUSTODY

Throughout the night Sylvia prayed for the safety of her daughter. She was desperate to know what had happened to her. At daylight, a police officer brought her what she considered to be a disgusting mug of tea and escorted her to a communal washroom to wash, which Sylvia declined to do. She also refused the dubious toothbrush she was offered until the officer produced one in a sealed packet.

Sylvia's thoughts were focused solely on Jane. When they had taken Sylvia away that night everyone else left too, abandoning Jane in an empty house in the middle of the night, alone, frightened, distressed and with her world shattered. The police, in their haste to secure an arrest, neglected to attend to Jane and her safety. They seemed to have forgotten that it was on her account that they had been summoned in the first place!

When Sylvia asked them what had happened to her daughter, they refused to tell her. She was so distraught at their lack of compassion that suddenly the floodgate of tears finally burst. However, the duty officers were unmoved – they had seen it all before. It was of no concern to them that they had left a frightened and vulnerable girl alone in the house after she had witnessed her tearful and distressed mother being taken away by the police. No one had taken responsibility for Jane and Sylvia was helpless to comfort her.

Sylvia was still in the cell when the day shift came on duty. She was hoping they would bring reassuring news of her daughter but no one appeared to be in any hurry to engage with her, despite the fact that it was obvious she was distressed. None of the staff on duty that morning felt inclined to talk to the prisoner who was securely locked in the cell, leaving her without further attention as they waited for the solicitor to arrive.

When the solicitor arrived, efficient and impersonal, he listened to Sylvia's account of the previous night's arrest. He was unperturbed and gave the impression that this would be a straightforward case without actually reassuring her.

Later that morning Sylvia was escorted to the magistrates' court for a so-called preliminary hearing, where the police officers made strenuous attempts to have her detained and remanded in custody pending further inquiries. Their punitive attitude was humiliating and heartless. However, the solicitor was well-acquainted with court proceedings and police tactics and he made a counter-submission to the magistrates. In view of his client's distressed state, he requested that she be admitted to a place of safety and suggested the local psychiatric hospital. The magistrates readily agreed and Sylvia was transferred to the hospital without delay before the police could make any further appeal.

GUARDIAN ANGEL

The hospital staff admitted Sylvia with compassion and reassurances, making her feel safe in their capable hands. Hers was a situation with which they were all too familiar.

The day she entered the hospital was strangely significant. Despite the cold terror gripping her heart, Sylvia sensed a change in the atmosphere. The news of her arrest had reached a wide audience already, including the local press, television and radio. There were people praying and interceding on her behalf and she could feel the effect of their combined prayers.

Had the police had their way, Sylvia would have been transferred to a remand centre several miles away for an indefinite period. Much to their annoyance, their plans had been thwarted by the solicitor's negotiations for her removal through the court from police custody to the supervision and care of medical professionals.

Sylvia, physically and mentally exhausted, passively allowed the ward staff to guide her through the day. By the evening, she gratefully retired to bed, relieved for a while to let go and rest in the calm stillness of her room.

Listening to the familiar sound of nurses bustling about the bedtime routine in the main ward reminded Sylvia of her own experiences as a hospital nurse. She was thankful for the privacy of a side ward and relieved that she did not have to spend the night in the company of strangers. Gradually the lights along the corridor were dimmed and peace descended on the ward.

After a while, as Sylvia lay in the dimly-lit room unable to sleep, she became aware of what she thought at first was a nurse. As she focused, she saw a figure resembling a nurse in the doorway surrounded by a gentle glow. In the stillness of the room the angelic being moved silently towards her bedside and reached out to touch her. At the angel's touch, Sylvia instantly fell into a deep sleep.

There are no words to describe fully the effect it had on Sylvia that night but she was convinced that she had been visited by an Angel whose presence and touch brought a supernatural peace and release.

THE CAVALRY ARRIVES

For the first few days in hospital Sylvia was alone in her hospital room, bereft of friends, family and fellowship. Then suddenly the 'cavalry' arrived on the scene in the form of a company of enthusiastic supporters – Christians, strangers and acquaintances who had heeded the call to rally round and come to her aid.

Their response and timely arrival gave Sylvia practical and spiritual support. It was exactly what she needed. Their cheerful presence brought hope lifting the dark cloud of fear and condemnation.

A SHINING LIGHT

One evening a few days after Sylvia's admission to the hospital, Lydia arrived upon the scene in the most extraordinary and unorthodox manner. Having arrived at the venue of a meeting in the town, and seeing that the place was in darkness, Lydia realized she had made a mistake about the date and began to make her way back home.

As she drove past the hospital, the words 'I was in prison and you did not visit Me' came into her mind. Struck by the severity of the words, she asked, 'When did I see You in prison and not visit You, Lord?' The words 'Sylvia is in the hospital and you have not visited her' were impressed upon her mind.

Although Lydia knew about Sylvia's admission to the hospital, she had only met her briefly at church and did not know her very well so, when she heard those words in her spirit, she was taken aback. Deeply impressed, she immediately turned the car around and drove back in the direction of the hospital.

She drove into the hospital grounds and headed towards the wards, even though it was well after visiting time. She had no idea where she was supposed to go; darkness was all around her. The wards were situated in individual buildings spread around the grounds.

'I don't know where to go,' she whispered, driving slowly along the shadowy drive. 'You will have to tell me where to go.'

She could see the outlines of the buildings against the dark sky ahead of her; each one was in darkness and they all looked the same, except for one solitary light shining over the door of one of them. She followed the light. Parking the car, she approached the building cautiously and knocked on the door, not knowing what to expect or what to say.

The door opened to reveal a puzzled nurse staring into the darkness.

'Hello, I know it's a bit late but I have come to see my friend,' Lydia said.

'Who is your friend?' the nurse asked suspiciously.

'Her name is Sylvia,' Lydia replied.

'Sylvia who?' the nurse enquired.

Well,' Lydia hesitated, 'I don't know her surname.'

'I am not sure she would want to see you,' replied the nurse, preparing to close the door.

Undeterred, Lydia persisted. 'Would you please ask her if she would see me?'

Reluctantly, the nurse agreed and disappeared inside, leaving Lydia waiting outside in the dark wondering what chance she had of being allowed in at that time of night.

After a while the mystified nurse returned, still doubtful about allowing her in. With growing confidence, Lydia persuaded the nurse to let her into the ward; eventually she condescended to do so and escorted her to Sylvia's bedside.

As they greeted each other, Sylvia and Lydia were astonished at this amazing, unpremeditated turn of events.

That night Lydia, a person Sylvia barely knew, stepped into her desperate situation when all seemed hopeless. That first unconventional meeting was the starting point of a strong and steadfast friendship that was to give strength to Sylvia's often flagging spirit over the subsequent challenging months. The strongest bond that held them together was their uncompromising faith.

Confined to life inside the hospital, Sylvia's outstanding problem was the distress her daughter was experiencing living with her father. He, together with his new partner, was considered by the authorities to be the responsible parent. Sylvia was convinced that the situation was painful and extremely damaging to her daughter's mental health, for Jane had witnessed the conflicts in their home over the years more than anyone else and knew all too well the mental and emotional pressures that had led to their present, disastrous situation.

When Sylvia's new friend Lydia heard of the unsuitable environment Jane was living in, she declared without the slightest hesitation, 'She must come to live with us!' And that is exactly what happened. With some difficulty, Lydia made arrangements with the social services for Jane to be removed forthwith from the unhappy and stressful situation with her father. The child was allowed to spend the rest of the time that mother and daughter were forced to be apart in the care of Lydia and her husband.

During the following months, Lydia stood by Sylvia in the most trying situations and shared her emotional roller-coaster ride. In turn, Lydia was supported not only by her husband but also by her faithful friend and confidante, Kelly.

The support team grew in strength and commitment over the following months. A continuous flow of new friends gathered around Sylvia, arriving miraculously from near and far to join in this most bizarre and incredible experience. They brought with them encouragement and support from churches and Christian groups across the region. Not only were they praying for Sylvia, they became the answer to their own prayers through their inspiring friendship.

One day a group from a neighbouring village arrived at the hospital with gifts, flowers and posters with which they decorated Sylvia's hospital room, enlivening the usually sombre atmosphere around her, much to the bewilderment of the ward staff. This group ensured that she had visitors every single day during the time she was confined to the hospital, trying their best to keep her occupied with their enthusiastic optimism.

Sylvia remained under the protection of the hospital for approximately three weeks, during which time she was able to regain control of her troubled mind. She was reassured that the 'place of safety' endorsed by the court was a binding legal directive that the police could not overturn, even though they continued to keep up the pressure. The police were frustrated that they were powerless to make progress with their case while Sylvia was in the care of the medical profession, which was actively contesting the case on her behalf. The senior consultant assured Sylvia that he would keep her in the hospital for as long as necessary despite police opposition.

The more Sylvia thought about the attitude of the police, the more she was at a loss to understand why they were spending so much time, energy and effort pursuing her case.

NO PLACE FOR PRIDE

During the time Sylvia was in hospital, there was one problem that may not have been obvious to anyone else: it was the problem of pride. Being arrested, imprisoned and then detained in a psychiatric hospital had an impact on Sylvia's well-being and self-esteem. Losing her respectable image was one of the most difficult challenges she had to face and there was no getting away from it: she had to deal with it.

To begin with, Sylvia had considered it a matter of professional courtesy that, as a nursing professional, she was given a private room when she was admitted. It came as a blow, therefore, when a few days after her admission the staff decided to transfer her to the ward with all the other patients. This move did not sit well with Sylvia and she wrestled with what she saw as a change in her status.

At first she was acutely uncomfortable living on a ward full of vulnerable patients, especially at night when some of them became restless and talked to themselves or to invisible companions. Some sang loudly, swore, shouted and generally created a commotion, keeping everyone awake. They often started arguments and provoked angry roars of retaliation up and down the ward. At times, some of the more unstable patients leapt out of bed to sort out the noisy ones themselves. It was certainly no place to sleep!

A few nights into her transfer to the general ward, Sylvia noticed that her disturbed, lonely and sad companions, with whom she now shared sleeping arrangements, seemed to settle down when she was with them. She found herself forgetting to be proud and self-centred and started to see them as individuals in need of love and acceptance. She often sat with them, comforting them and listening to their confused and sometimes tragic stories as they tumbled out unrestrained during the long hours of the night.

To her surprise, as she listened she felt a tenderness rising up within her. Forgetting herself, she began to understand and care more about them and their need for peace in their tormented lives. And, in so doing, her self-centred pride gave way to love and compassion.

NO EASY BATTLE

Eventually, as it became obvious to the doctors that it was impractical to confine Sylvia in the hospital any longer, the consultant applied to the court stating that it was 'in his patient's best interests' to continue her recovery and rehabilitation at home.

Once the consultant's application was approved, Sylvia was allowed to leave the hospital while still under his care. This new arrangement antagonised the police further as it became obvious that they had been outmanoeuvred. With Sylvia remaining under the care and jurisdiction of the doctors, even as an outpatient, their plans had been thwarted once again.

Amazingly, the police maintained their aggressive determination to make life difficult for Sylvia. In the circumstances, she was forced to consider whether the fact that her husband who was a serving police officer was a contributing factor. Maybe there had been rumours that he could have been implicated in her desperate reaction to the breakdown of their marriage. Maybe the police had closed ranks.

Based on all that was happening, Sylvia knew that this was more than just a routine criminal case; however implausible, it seemed that she was the subject of a personal attack. She was not oblivious to the implications ; this was no easy battle and she needed all the help she could get. Miraculously, help appeared every time she needed it.

With the encouragement and support of the medical and nursing professionals, Sylvia left the hospital to return home. It felt good to be released from the confines of the hospital, even though she was still on bail. However, being at home with no legal access to her daughter, which was one of the bail conditions, was extremely stressful.

Jane made straight for home as soon as she knew her mother had been released from the hospital. Sylvia had to explain to her that it would not be possible for her daughter to come home whenever she wanted as it would put Sylvia in danger of breaking the bail conditions and be re-arrested.

Despite their deep frustration, they devised a plan for Jane to return home whenever her mother was away. To that end, Sylvia took advantage of two 'boltholes' that were available to her, enabling Jane to come home whenever her mother was away. Although still forced to continue living apart, they were at least able to talk to each other by phone, and the opportunity to be at home in familiar surroundings, although still living with Lydia and her husband, brought some comfort to Jane.

One of the boltholes was the home of Sylvia's brother, Arthur, in Yorkshire. He and his wife welcomed her with open arms, supporting her and accompanying her to and from Stafford for the various court appearances. They made every effort to keep life as normal as possible during her stay with them.

The other safe place was a rectory in Lancashire, the benefice of their old friend Peter. This particular contact was yet another demonstration of someone learning miraculously of Sylvia's arrest and coming to her aid. Peter traced her to her brother's home in Yorkshire through several telephone links. Upon hearing about the desperate situation she was in, he and his wife became loyal supporters and counsellors and offered her a place in their home at the rectory.

The rectory became a sanctuary, a place to come and go whenever Sylvia needed a break from the pressures at home. Often, during the most stressful periods when the weeks and months dragged by and drained her physical and emotional energy, and when the effort to maintain a brave face overwhelmed her, Peter and his family did everything in their power to hold things together. They surrounded Sylvia with their love when all she could do was sob as though her heart would break. These kind, compassionate friends ministered to Sylvia with infinite wisdom and patience, steadying her course whenever the storms raged within and without. There were times when it seemed as though there was nothing on earth that could lift her, but at such times Heaven came down in their home.

The occasions Sylvia spent at the rectory opened doors into spiritual realms she had never encountered before. Although they were far beyond her comprehension, she was undeniably in kind and loving hands.

NO FOOD ALLOWED!

Inevitably Sylvia had to return to her empty home to observe the bail conditions. Jane was finding it hard living apart from her mother and the strain was beginning to tell. By now she had returned to her old school, where she had the support of her friends and teachers, but the stress was having a detrimental effect upon her health and well-being.

Supervision by a social worker made life even more difficult and humiliating for both mother and daughter. Officially they were only supposed to see each other under supervision. The social worker allocated to them was particularly insensitive and difficult; she sat between them during the visits, making their ordeal even more stressful. She forbade Sylvia giving Jane anything to eat during the visits, such as chocolate or snacks, informing her that it was not allowed. She was obviously inexperienced and clung to the letter of the law. Her rigid attitude, without a trace of empathy, was deeply wounding.

When the probation officer allocated to Sylvia's case heard of this, he volunteered to undertake the supervisory role. He chose to sit in his car during the visits, indicating his full support. With his experience and intuitive approach, he considered the social worker's attitude and rigorous restrictions unnecessary. Sylvia was greatly encouraged by his faith in her. She remembered his kindness during that difficult time with much gratitude, and carried those memories in her heart forever.

UNDER SURVEILLANCE

Although Sylvia was now free to travel wherever she wished, there were other challenges to deal with. Living at home attracted the attention of the media and made her more exposed to public attention, making her feel more vulnerable. There were updates in the press every time she appeared in court, and public and media interest increased when the date for the trial was set for September, nine months from the day of her arrest.

Sylvia had been suspended from work as a matter of course, but she had the support of her employers. Both her immediate and senior managers supported her and maintained regular contact but the fact that all her colleagues knew about her embarrassing situation was difficult to bear.

As the weeks and months stretched out before her, Sylvia was acutely aware that she was under constant surveillance by the police and the press. Neighbours and acquaintances found it difficult to relate to her; for the most part, they avoided direct contact with her as she ran the gauntlet of their inquisitive stares on a daily basis.

It was not an easy situation; normal life was on hold as far as Sylvia was concerned. Without the faithful support of friends bolstering her up and encouraging her, she would not have had the courage to endure the daily ordeal of opening her front door each morning.

At times when things became even more difficult, Sylvia was warmed and encouraged by letters and cards from her 'mothers' – the women who knew her as their health visitor and had had the benefit of the support she had given to them and their families. Clients and colleagues from the past, who had seen news reports about her arrest in the press and on the television, contacted her with good wishes and kind words of encouragement.

One day at the local post office, during a particularly depressing phase, as the postmaster pushed Sylvia's stamps towards her over the counter, he said with a deadpan expression, 'Don't let the buggers get you down!' His sentiments were heart-warming. That well-intended phrase gave her renewed hope and later she would recall those words with a smile and tears of gratitude.

As the date for the trial drew near, the interaction between the solicitor and the court officials quickened pace. Sylvia was excluded from the protracted legal processes as she had nothing more to contribute.

The police continued to make their presence felt; wherever she went she was aware them. She had the distinct impression that they were waiting for her to do something incriminating that they could use as further evidence of her guilt.

From the little information she received from her solicitor, it appeared that the police were having some difficulty making their case to the Director of Public Prosecutions (DPP). The charge, stipulating that she was guilty of 'administering a noxious substance to a juvenile', did not seem to impress the DPP who increased the pressure on the police to produce something more substantial – but there seemed to be little they could do.

Sylvia's solicitor engaged a barrister to represent her and remained optimistic. As the proceedings gathered momentum, Sylvia's confidence was slowly increasing, and she began to feel optimistic.

THE FLIGHT

Towards the end of the summer, Sylvia was summoned to the local Crown Court for yet another interim court appearance. Lydia accompanied her to the hearing but, as time dragged on, she had to leave to collect her children from school. She was not happy leaving Sylvia alone, but had no other option.

Sylvia assured her that she would be fine; it was just another formality, she was not anticipating anything she couldn't handle. Reluctantly Lydia hurried away to collect the children, leaving Sylvia feeling calm and relatively confident.

When the formalities ended, Sylvia headed towards the exit at the front of the courthouse. She was just about to descend the steps into the busy market square when a dark figure suddenly jumped out in front of her, brandishing a large long-lens camera. Startled, she hesitated for a fraction of a second. Then, pushing past him, she ran frantically down the steps into the main shopping precinct in an attempt to lose him in the crowds milling in front of the courthouse.

Her pursuer followed, expertly fixing his camera on her as he ran. It was apparent that he was prepared for this and not easily deterred. To shake him off, Sylvia opened her umbrella. Holding it close, she shielded her face as she zig-zagged as fast as she could between the afternoon shoppers.

Her would-be assailant was gaining on her. Seeing nowhere to escape, in desperation she ran across the market square towards an open shop door. Without a backward glance, she raced straight through the shop, out of the rear exit and through the park towards the railway station as though her life depended on it.

At the taxi rank, she jumped into a taxi and yelled out Lydia's address, instructing the taxi driver to drive quickly. Sensing the urgency in her voice, he drove off with no questions asked. Reaching Lydia's house, Sylvia ran through the front door, trembling and breathless, wondering what that had all been about!

She soon found out. The next day, still recovering from the fright of the previous afternoon, she returned to her friend's house. She let herself in and walked in to find Lydia standing in the kitchen, holding the telephone in her hand as though rooted to the spot. Sylvia was immediately alarmed at the expression on her face 'What's the matter?' she cried, dreading the reply.

'They have changed the charge to attempted murder!' Lydia exclaimed in disbelief.

ATTEMPTED MURDER

Sylvia fell to the floor as though she had been dealt a body blow. Alarmed, Lydia called the doctor. Shocked to the core, fear gripped Sylvia's heart as her world crumbled once again. The confidence she had regained over the past few weeks disappeared in an instant. Frozen with terror, she had no strength left to overcome this latest blow. How could she stand against the brute force of those who were using their indisputable power and authority to destroy her?

Quickly recovering, Lydia stepped into the breach and took control of the situation, rallying prayer support. The battle had reached a new level altogether. The news spread far and wide as spiritually strong reinforcements rallied round to counteract this latest attack. Meanwhile Lydia accompanied Sylvia home and stayed with her that night, refusing to allow her to face this latest crisis alone.

The police had pursued the original charge of administering a noxious substance to a juvenile against Sylvia for months, but it had proved insufficient to be brought to court. They were therefore obliged to come up with this new charge. It was shocking, sensational and guaranteed to grab attention and influence public opinion. The police renewed their efforts to substantiate their false claims even further, enlarging upon the original report made on the night of the arrest.

False incriminating statements such as 'She has been plying the child with sleeping pills and sherry', which Sylvia had heard a police officer relaying into his mobile phone from her kitchen that night, were significant factors in their investigation. The allegations had been recorded without proof, let alone following an interview with the juvenile in question who had been hiding in her bedroom, terrified by the commotion downstairs and had been left alone and unattended when her mother had been arrested.

Those statements, given by an officer of the law, were presumed to be the truth based on his position of authority as an enforcer of the law. It was frightening that such malicious accusations made by a police officer within minutes of entering the house, without any evidence to support his claims, could have such a devastating effect. Sylvia was in no position to contradict him. His opinion had been supposedly informed and influenced by the doctor, who had arrived at the same time as the police, having previously alerted them to attend a crime scene on the basis of what the churchwarden had told him over the phone.

With the news of the new charge, the case against Sylvia changed dramatically and took on an entirely new perspective. Her situation looked more serious than ever. The prospect of a successful outcome for her seemed impossible and she was in a desperate place. That night she reached her lowest point and saw no way out

Remarkably, the following morning when Lydia had to leave for home, Sylvia woke up with a determination to fight back This was in complete contrast to the fear that had paralysed her the day before and was reinforced by the same extraordinary peace that the angel had brought her that first night in the hospital. It was time to make a stand. She realised that even in this hopeless situation she had a choice. She could crumble under the threat of being branded a potential murderer or, with the help of God, refuse to be defeated.

NAMED BLAMED AND SHAMED

The next day the newspapers and the media were full of the new charges. As Sylvia faced the new round of publicity, she recalled a newspaper article she once read reporting a similar situation. *Named, Blamed and Shamed*, the headlines had proclaimed, blaring out the shocking news. Some unfortunate individual's name blazed across the front pages of the newspapers and intimate details of their life were broadcast from television and radio stations for all to see.

What had previously been private became public property, open to all, leaving no place to hide. The general public might not have heard of this person before, but now they knew not only the accused's name but all the details of their private life. They had become the subject of criticism and prejudice, as though knowing their name and the accusations against them had given people the right to judge them. Their name became familiar to everyone; tossed around, it was suddenly the focus of gossip and speculation, vilified by the ignorant and misinformed. They become public property, their reputation torn to shreds and every detail exposed, regardless of whether they were innocent or guilty, or even if the details were relevant. The accused individual lost control over their identity and self-respect – the most personal part of their being that validated their self-worth. It wrecked their world.

Being innocent did not protect them from disgrace or humiliation in the glare of public scrutiny. Worst of all, the opinion of the general public would not necessarily have been their own; to a large extent, their opinions were the result of whatever the media had told them and that, in turn, depended on the slant the media put on the information. The truth is often, as they say, 'lost in translation'.

This was the situation into which Sylvia was thrown – a maelstrom of malevolence, confusion and doubt. But as the pressure increased, so did her resolve to be undefeated even though it looked as though, in the glare of the publicity, she had no power to defeat such a strong enemy.

The officers on her case had denied the truth when it did not fit the charge. They found the solution by altering the facts. The new charge was calculated to mislead and deceive. They were confident about their ability to overrule the protests of an undeniably disadvantaged individual. Their statements seemed more credible and carried more weight than those of the accused – a fifty-year-old woman who they considered incapable of defending herself against their well-documented allegations.

Indisputably the police had the upper hand. The fact that there was no substance to their claims was of no consequence. The bottle of sherry in the dining room and the paracetamol tablets in the kitchen cupboard were good starting points, and the fact that the accused had sleeping tablets in her bedroom was a bonus!

It seemed inconceivable that such a gross misrepresentation of the facts could form the basis of an arrest with so little evidence. One did not need an expert to explain what led to the situation that night. A preliminary assessment by a doctor would have revealed that Sylvia was an individual in the throes of a mental crisis and in need of immediate attention. Instead, the situation was exacerbated by the incompetence and negligence of a medical practitioner who cruelly chose to hand her over to the police, when in reality there was no evidence of a crime.

The press had been tipped off about the new charge and the pressure increased each day as the trial date approached. As interest in the case escalated, Sylvia became headline news again. Remembering once more the premonition when everything around her was exploding, She took comfort in knowing that she came out of the devastation unscathed. Even so, it was hard to maintain a positive attitude and every day she struggled to maintain her composure.

THE TRIAL

Sylvia's brother, Arthur, and his wife, Norma, arrived from Yorkshire on Tuesday, the day before the trial at the Birmingham Crown Court. They were anxious on her behalf and put a great deal of effort into distracting her from the reports on the BBC evening news. None of them had an appetite that evening as they made stilted and carefully light-hearted conversation, avoiding the very thing that was dominating their thoughts.

That evening a deputation arrived from the church Sylvia had been attending for most of the nine months she was on bail. They came to offer their support and prayers. During the months Sylvia had been attending their church, they had not found it easy to reconcile their views about the dilemma of a Christian in their midst breaking their marriage vows and, according to their understanding, stepping out of God's will. Sylvia wondered why it had not occurred to them to enquire about the possibility of extenuating circumstances, or why they had not given her the opportunity to explain. Perhaps she had been asking too much of them by expecting their unconditional support, even though there was no evidence in her demeanour that indicated a rebellious or wilful spirit.

She understood their problem and received their sincere gesture. They left with a 'word from the Lord' in the form of a scripture from the Bible: 'In quietness and in confidence shall be your strength'. They meant well, and the scripture was supposed to encourage her, but she had the impression that they were not optimistic about the outcome of the case. The situation was so unreal; everyone was on edge and this was unknown territory for all of them. Ironically, she had previously hoped for their support, but now, at the most critical time on the eve of the trial, she had no need of their fearful counsel!

Surprisingly, in view of the circumstances, Sylvia slept soundly that night. It could have been the result of extreme exhaustion or it may have been that, once again, an extraordinary sense of peace surrounded her. She felt sorry for Arthur and Norma, who were trying to help her while struggling to control their own emotions. Preparing for that first day of the trial, Sylvia was incredibly calm, ready to face whatever the day held.

BIRMINGHAM CROWN COURT

DAY ONE

Accompanied by her brother, Sylvia arrived early at Birmingham Crown Court after what seemed to have been a long and difficult night for her brother and sister-in-law. Outside the court, they were greeted by a crowd of reporters. Her daughter, Jane, arrived separately, accompanied by Lydia and the social worker, but Sylvia did not see them arrive.

Arthur, Norma and a group of friends were directed to the public gallery, while Sylvia was escorted to a private office and introduced for the first time to the defending barrister. Decisive and self-assured, he wasted no time in outlining his plan of action, stating that he did not require Sylvia to take the stand if she did not wish to do so.

Although previously she had been fearful at the prospect of defending herself in open court, now she was determined to have her say. She was not going to miss this opportunity. As before, a distinctive quiet resolve rose from somewhere deep within her; she felt a strong and almost exhilarating boldness and affirmed unhesitatingly that she would take the stand.

Before leaving his office, the barrister added a caveat: he said there was the possibility that the case would be dropped at the last minute but they would not know until the judge gave his decision immediately before opening the proceedings.

Sylvia left the barrister's office. Finding Lydia, she shared this latest, unexpected turn of events with her. Was she to be reprieved at the last minute? Was the case to be abandoned? There was nothing they could do but wait and see.

They did not have to wait long; almost immediately they were called to take their places in the courtroom. They were bitterly disappointed and parted reluctantly, deflated and confused. Lydia joined friends and supporters with Arthur as they hurried to the public gallery. Sylvia was accompanied to the dock by a police officer. She noted that the officer had handcuffs jangling from her waist as she sat beside her throughout the proceedings.

The session commenced with the swearing in of the jury, followed by the Judge's opening remarks and his instructions to the jury. The prosecuting barrister made his preliminary submissions to the court and the arresting police officer was called to provide his evidence for the prosecution. This was followed by Sylvia's barrister making a clear and concise submission to the court then questions to the witnesses.

Despite the serious charge against her, Sylvia found the proceedings fascinating and completely absorbing, and was surprised at her own composure. The first day ended in an orderly manner, giving little indication of how the hearing was progressing.

As they made their exit, they ran the gauntlet of journalists outside the building. The drive home was subdued; they were overwhelmed and exhausted. Back home, Arthur and Norma made sure Sylvia did not see or hear any of the news on the television. She was glad to retire to bed and they were relieved from protecting her from the outside world.

They were dreading the second day of the trial but Sylvia, still remarkably calm, once again fell into a deep sleep. It was as though she were being protected by a strong invisible force and held steady by unseen hands.

BIRMINGHAM CROWN COURT

DAY TWO

On the second day there was a larger media presence waiting outside the court as Sylvia and her brother made their way into the building. They were intimidated by the sight of the group of journalists and reporters who were bent on creating a sensational story. They pushed their way through, trying their best to ignore them.

Day Two consisted of the prosecuting and defence counsels presenting their cases and hearing the witnesses, including the police. Steve was also called for questioning. Sylvia was surprised to note that he did not receive sympathetic questioning by either the defence or prosecuting barristers; it was obvious that he was uncomfortable.

When Jane was brought to the dock, the judge spoke kindly to her, making it easy for her to answer the questions. The prosecuting and defence counsels also addressed her briefly and sensitively. Finally the Judge summed up the session and asked her directly, 'Let us get this straight. Do you think your mother was trying to murder you?' When she answered with an emphatic and exasperated, 'No,' the Judge turned to the jury and said, 'There you have it!'

There was a distinct atmosphere of empathy in the courtroom, as though everyone wanted to show their support for this naive schoolgirl in the dock whose artless answers revealed her obvious innocence and vulnerability.

This empathy continued when it was Sylvia's turn to testify. Even the questions from the prosecution were sympathetic – no trick questions, no pressure and no attempt to unnerve her. She did not feel intimidated in any way; in fact, she felt extraordinarily composed. There was an absence of the impartial formality she had expected in a courtroom; there appeared to be a climate of favour and goodwill in the public gallery, too. An air of suppressed anticipation permeated the courtroom as though everyone had a personal interest in the outcome.

As they left the court that day, Sylvia was filled with anticipation and impatient for the next day to arrive. Thankfully, she noticed that her companions were just slightly less anxious!

BIRMINGHAM CROWN COURT

DAY THREE

By the third day, the waiting press were out in force and in a state of high expectation, anticipating a dramatic outcome. By now, Sylvia and Arthur were able to pass through the crowd of journalists converging on the pavement outside the entrance with more confidence, refusing to be threatened or distracted by them.

The morning session began with the Judge opening the proceeding by summing up the presentations from the prosecution and defence barristers before instructing the jury to retire to make their decision. As they filed out of the courtroom to await the jury's verdict, it was still only halfway through the morning. Sylvia and her anxious companions waited in the restaurant, drinking coffee and wondering how long they would have to wait.

To everyone's surprise, they were called back into the courtroom in less than hour. After the initial buzz of excitement, the chatter emanating from the gallery subsided and a hush descended on the court, as though everyone were holding their breath and waiting to hear the jury's decision.

The judge asked the foreman if they had reached their decision and the foreman replied, 'Yes.' The Judge then asked if it was a unanimous decision, and the foreman affirmed that it was.

'What is your decision?' enquired the Judge.

After a brief pause, the foreman replied, 'Not guilty.'

A collective sigh of relief rippled through the courtroom and a variety of exclamations of gratitude to God could be heard from the gallery. The judge accepted the verdict and concluded with his summing-up statement and closing remarks.

The court rose as the Judge made his exit, at which point the police officer standing next to Sylvia turned to her and simply said with a smile, 'You are free to go now,' and left.

Sylvia felt no inclination to move; the enormity of that moment was overwhelming. It was all over! She was free! Overjoyed, she stood rooted to the spot not knowing what to do, but the cheering from the public gallery left her in no doubt that she was indeed free to go.

Outside the courtroom, she was greeted by an enthusiastic crowd; she was hugged until she could hardly breathe! The BBC cameras were waiting on the pavement ready to capture her first reaction. Dazed and bewildered, at their request she voiced her relief, adding that she and Jane had had the most difficult and harrowing experience owing to the unreasonable and irresponsible treatment they had received from the police.

Exonerated from any criminal charge, Sylvia was free; but after nine months of inexpressible pain and persecution, the damage was done. The wounds were deep. and her life was changed forever. She would never be the same again.

Reunited with friends and family, she left the excited well-wishers and hastily returned home to collect Jane. Some of the paparazzi hung on and followed them all the way back to Stafford. They later discovered a lone reporter crouching in a corner of the restaurant where they had gathered for a celebratory lunch but by that time they were past caring what the press were up to!

PICKING UP THE PIECES

In the days that followed, friends and family discussed the outcome and the reason why the Judge had pronounced that the trial should go ahead. They agreed that he had made his decision in Sylvia's best interests; with the not guilty verdict, there would be no room for further speculation about whether she was guilty or not. They knew too well that if the trial had been halted, there would have been the possibility of people insinuating 'no smoke without fire'. They were grateful for the judge's wise decision and for the common sense of the jury that proved there was no room for doubt.

Finally Jane and Sylvia were free to resume their normal routine but their post-trial life was far from normal after such a damaging experience. Their first reaction was one of relief but inevitably they were still bearing the consequences of the whole traumatic episode, both mentally and emotionally.

It was at this point that Jane, finding it difficult to adjust, blanked out her memory of the past nine months. Sylvia was left to cope with her alone when, in reality, she was in no state to help. Today both Jane and Sylvia would have been offered counselling but at the time the impact of such an experience, even if it had been recognized, was not addressed.

They were thankful that the ordeal that had separated them for so long was over. In a state of post-traumatic shock, they endeavoured to support each other without any outside assistance. Their well-meaning friends thought it best to let them get on with adjusting to normal life by themselves when, in fact, that was the time Sylvia and Jane needed them most. They were still vulnerable and fragile, struggling to come to terms with all that they had endured.

Outwardly Sylvia maintained her composure but the haunting and recurring memories of the past year hung over her like a dark cloud. Now that she had time to reflect, she found it difficult to come to terms with the fact that, when she had been at her lowest point and in the greatest need, she was failed by the doctor on call that fateful night – the very person who could have saved her from the cruel absurdity that followed. The malicious and sensational misrepresentation by the police on the night she was arrested and the nine months on bail had further weakened her inner reserves. Now, in the aftermath, she was struggling to regain a sense of self-worth, carrying an undeserved sense of guilt and questioning whether she would ever feel truly free and respected again. After twenty-five years of loneliness and heartache resulting in a mental breakdown, she could not forget that she had been branded a criminal and, even worse, a potential murderer!

Everyone expected Sylvia to return to work without delay; they were eager to see everything back to normal even though she was far from ready. She did not feel up to the challenge of facing the people who had distanced themselves from her during her absence from her job.

Unaware of her misgivings, well-meaning friends thought that it was time for Sylvia to start enjoying life again They were relieved that the ordeal was over but they underestimated the extent of the emotional trauma she had sustained over the past nine months. They were completely oblivious to the fact that she was dreading taking that first step back into the world of work again.

However, responding to their well-meaning advice, Sylvia returned to work shortly after the trial ended. It was far more challenging than anyone had imagined. Re-establishing relationships was easier said than done. She was apprehensive and lacked confidence, fearful of meeting her colleagues again. It took all the courage she could muster to turn up for work on that first day.

The prospect of meeting everyone was made more difficult by the absence of any formal help or support from her employers. The nurse manager had advised staff to refrain from approaching Sylvia on the subject of her ordeal when it would have been a relief to talk and be reassured of their goodwill and support.

Sylvia had not had contact with the majority of her colleagues during her absence. She was grateful for the few who warmly welcomed her return and disappointed by the others who were wary and kept their distance, unsure of how to handle her. Their indifferent attitude added to her discomfort and sense of failure. Her relationship with many of them had been purely on a professional basis so when the news broke of her arrest, it came as a shock. They had learned the details of her breakdown through the press and television. Remembering this at the point of her return made Sylvia feel embarrassed and alienated, knowing that her personal and private life had finally been exposed.

As a health visitor, Sylvia was trained to help the families she served in overcoming their problems – not only the practical mother-and-baby issues but also their emotional and mental concerns. Sharing her own personal problems with anyone was another matter; she had become used to keeping her own counsel.

It was a bittersweet experience to receive kindness and good wishes from the general public and, at the same time, experience the lack of support from her fellow workers, some of whom she had considered to be friends. However, she sympathized with those who found the situation difficult for she also found re-establishing relationships challenging. Nevertheless, although returning to work filled her with dread, there was no way of avoiding it.

Family and friends continued to be encouraging, relieved that the experience that had turned all their lives upside down was over and done with. But for Sylvia it was not easy; for a while she was so unsettled that she considered leaving the area.

But she knew that she could not run away and in the end she stayed, accepting the fact that she would have to live with the memories wherever she went. That sad night when she had poured out her dark and troubled thoughts in the incriminating letters, would stay with her but the pain of exposing herself and her family to a whole kaleidoscope of catastrophic events need not dominate her future.

Trying to put the situation into some sort of perspective, Sylvia reflected on the news currently circulating around the world media following the dramatic cave rescue of twelve junior football team members and their coach in Thailand. The group had been led into the cave by their coach and been trapped for ten days in the cave due to sudden monsoon floods. She tried to imagine the regret and anguish of the team coach who had made the fateful decision to enter the cave during the monsoon season, the repercussions of which none of them would ever forget! Undoubtedly he would live with the memory of his disastrous decision for the rest of his life too.

A NEW BEGINING

Time does not stand still. After the dust settled, Sylvia made every effort to move on and put the past behind her. She was determined not to be bound by the trivial things she had previously considered important, paying more attention now to the things that were worthwhile and separating the positive from the negative.

But some issues remained unresolved. She continued to wrestle with the situation concerning the doctor at the centre of her ordeal. She had received advice about pressing charges on the grounds of professional negligence. The local branch of the Medical Complaints Board and the local Member of Parliament advised her to press charges of unprofessional conduct but the issue was sapping her energy and, in light of all that she had already endured, she let it drop. It was of no consequence anymore.

She had no doubt that the police had a case to answer too, but knowing that their attempts to convict her had failed so miserably was satisfaction enough and that issue went unchallenged too.

After the trial, the divorce was finalized and her divided family went their separate ways. Together with Susan and Jane, Sylvia looked to the future without any support from their extended family apart from her faithful brother, Arthur. Sylvia and Jane remained in Stafford, having lost contact with most of their friends in Salford. The rest of her siblings were totally indifferent to their situation and her former brothers-in-law cut Sylvia and Jane out of their lives altogether.

Susan and her new husband were now living in Canterbury. Committed to new occupations and constrained by distance, they were unable to provide practical support. Nor did they receive any support from their extended family as they too came to terms with all they had experienced over the past year.

Susan had the difficult task of keeping in touch with both her parents and suffered the consequences of such a frustrating arrangement.

Jane eventually emerged from her teenage years outwardly unscathed but, in reality, in the aftermath of her traumatic experience during her adolescence she continued to struggle with unresolved, deep-seated emotional issues. In the absence of any professional support, she went through several rough patches emotionally and for a long time could not be reconciled with her father, finding it hard to forgive him for all the unhappiness he had caused. Sylvia looked sadly at her friends' happy marriages and became resigned to the fact that there seemed to be no true resolution for any of them.

Eventually, as Steve entered his seventies, his health began to deteriorate; after a prolonged series of illnesses, he died. Sylvia was taken aback at the impact the news of his death had on her. She was overwhelmed by the strength of emotions released in floods of tears that had been held back for all the years since their divorce. She experienced a profound grief as the sad memories poured out unrestrained – searingly painful and yet unexplained. She thought she had dealt with the sadness and heartache and was therefore unprepared for the intensity of her reaction to her former husband's death.

THE MISSING PIECE

After the funeral, Susan and Sylvia met to discuss the last days before Steve died, communicating freely for the first time about his behaviour. Over the years Susan had been fiercely protective towards her father. Now at last they were able to voice the concerns that had baffled them for so long. They began to share long-held suspicions and gradually, with the help of an experienced autism researcher aided by current medical practice into Autism Syndrome Disorder (ASD), they discovered the secret that had held them bound in ignorance for so long. What they discovered was profoundly disturbing and changed everything!

The explanation was surprisingly simple. It was truly a 'Gestalt' moment: the theory that explains a situation, where one significant fact emerges to explain the whole and provides the vital link. It was as though someone had suddenly produced the missing piece of a jigsaw puzzle, after which everything begins to fall into place.

The facts revealed that Steve had been on the autistic spectrum and had remained undiagnosed as a child and throughout his adult years. They were shocked and dismayed to learn that he had been suffering from a condition about which little was known before the 1950s. Autism had only been recognized in recent years as a developmental brain disorder resulting from complex genetic factors, its cause unknown thus far. As with Steve, many children entered adulthood without being diagnosed.

ASD encompasses a wide range of disabilities that affect each individual differently. It is marked by deficits in the development of social and communication skills and in understanding and maintaining relationships. The condition is characterised by the inability to show empathy or understand non-verbal communication. Individuals with ASD find participating in social activities challenging, the symptoms of which made life extremely difficult for Steve and Sylvia throughout their marriage.

A wealth of information regarding the signs of autism is available today. It is relatively easy to diagnose now by a trained practitioner but in the 1940s and 1950s, the years when Steve was growing up, it was still a mystery. This explained the confusion experienced by his mother regarding his development and behaviour as a child, and his inability to function normally in non-verbal situations as an adult.

It is possible that his mother's secretive and rigid control over him was her way of dealing with him and was probably a contributing factor that exacerbated his condition. Her attitude may have been the result of her misunderstanding of mental-health issues and the fear of mental institutions passed down through the generations.

Sadly, ASD was a term not yet used. The signs and symptoms of Steve's condition were not apparent to casual observers in the 1960s when Sylvia and Steve were married, nor was it recognized as a diagnosis by the medical profession.

REVELATION AND TEARS

For days after discovering the secret of the missing piece in their relationship Sylvia struggled to come to terms with the shocking revelation and tried to make sense of the information that had evaded her for so long and ruined their marriage. At last she was able to understand all the misconceptions she had had about Steve's challenging behaviour, the man she had grown to believe as insensitive and uncaring.

The tragedy was that he had gone to his grave without his condition being acknowledged or diagnosed and she had spent years demanding behaviour from him that he was incapable of providing. With hindsight, she began to understand what a struggle life must have been for him too, living without recognition or support and with no understanding from her whatsoever.

Autism had robbed him of his capacity to develop and mature normally so it was no wonder that he had had problems understanding what was expected of him. They had faced conflicts and misunderstandings constantly throughout their married life and at times their stress levels had been unbearably high. Sylvia had been forced to take a leading role in the marriage out of necessity and resented it because she thought her husband was neglectful and indifferent.

Today, with the advantages of modern medical practices, there would be support for both of them and Sylvia would have risen to the challenge, believing that love conquers all. By understanding the problem, she could have helped Steve live a happy and fulfilling life and perhaps they could have found happiness together.

PEACE LIKE A RIVER

Finally, in the light of the new revelations, and the stranglehold over her broken, for the first time in many years Sylvia experienced a true sense of freedom, a freedom that brought a wonderful peace, the missing peace!

Discovering the secret and its corroding influence over her and Steve, was the catalyst to forgiving him unreservedly. It opened the floodgates in other areas long forgotten but whose power, like a curse, had marred her every waking hour. For the longest time, she thought that she had forgiven Steve but somewhere deep down she had been bound by invisible ties. Now light came shining into all the dark places and a multitude of associated painful memories poured out unrestrained.

The freedom she now felt overwhelmed her, the pain of the past rapidly evaporating as if she was waking from a bad dream. Relief flooded through her whole being as the lack of forgiveness, with its evil intent, fled like darkness driven out at the dawning of the day.

Casting her mind back over the years, she understood now that Sarah had raised her children in a time when research into complex medical problems, particularly in the area of mental health and genetic disorders, was still in its infancy. Without the advantages of modern medicine she had coped as best she could with her son's disorder without any professional support. Like a mother hen, she had instinctively protected her offspring.

Now, as the healing tears flowed, Sylvia saw how much she needed not only to forgive but to be forgiven, for without doubt her own attitude had hindered Sarah's efforts to hold things together in exceedingly difficult circumstances.

Sylvia was seeing things now that she had never even considered before, not only how hurtful her attitude towards Sarah had been but how much she had hurt Steve too. She was overwhelmed at the revelation of how her attitude had deteriorated over the years. She had allowed her heart to harden and had lost sight of her love for him, considering herself to be the injured party! Perhaps if she had been more willing to understand him, they could have surmounted the difficulties they encountered, believing that love counters a multitude of sins even in the most frustrating situations.

Steve's condition had clearly contributed to the events that diverted them away from accomplishing their dreams. Sylvia saw how their lives had changed when, as a probationer in the Pentecostal Church, he had been denied ordination because of his inability to cope with the demands on a spiritual leader. They were both hurt and disappointed and she was sad to see that Steve had struggled to express how he felt. At the time she had tried to help him overcome the rejection but it had been difficult. In the light of what she now knew, it was obvious that there had been a significant reason why Steve was refused ordination and that the church authorities were ill-equipped to deal with it.

Still reeling from the revelations, Sylvia could not escape the painful memories that continued to dominate her thoughts, especially memories of the people who had contributed so devastatingly to her already traumatic circumstances. But within days everything began to change. Previously she had been held back by the unhappy memories and the enigma surrounding her relationship with Steve. Now, as her mind cleared, she was amazed at the magnitude of the transformation taking place and the wonderful freedom it brought. She was free now from the self-condemnation and guilt and all the negative thoughts that had held her captive over the years. She remembered with gratitude the friends who had stood by her and the strangers who came to her aid in the darkest times, holding her up when she was too distressed and frightened to stand alone.

TRAGEDY TO TRIUMPH

Sylvia's tragic experience is not unique; such situations are being repeated continually throughout the world where countless individuals are facing traumatic and life-threatening persecution.

There are many instances of shattered lives displayed on our television screens every day. Sylvia's story has been told from a Christian point of view, but there are many brave individuals across the world of different faiths and convictions who suffer persecution, abuse and discrimination for who they are and for the things they hold dear. They courageously pay the price for what they believe and, incredibly in many cases, they forgive their tormentors.

There are many remarkable instances of those who have emerged from tragedy to triumph and have moved on to live happy and fulfilling lives. As Joel Osteen, the pastor of the Lakewood Church in America, would say: 'This is the key.' For all of us, the key is in many instances the giving and receiving forgiveness heralding a profound sense of peace

DESTINED TO WIN

Today Sylvia can see that it is in her power to turn her back on the past and recreate her life, proving that no matter how distressing the experience, recovery is possible and restoration a reality. She has lived through the futility of dwelling on the misfortunes of the past and is grateful for a future of opportunities for happiness.

Her story does not end here; it is still unfolding. She has learned not to count herself out because of the lost years or yesterday's mistakes. The events recounted here are just a moment in time; the past is over and tomorrow is a new day. Yesterday has come and gone; it 'came to pass' and, like the seasons, there will always be change and another chance to start again. It is never too late.

Regardless of whether you are blessed in a season of success and contentment or bound by discouragement and depression, it is likely that somewhere along the way there have been failures, regrets or lost opportunities in your life that have caused you to doubt or lose hope.

Remember that yesterday is gone forever and is beyond your control. You cannot undo a single act you have performed or take back a single word you have spoken. Tomorrow, the sun will rise – either in all its splendour or hidden behind the clouds – but until it does, you have no stake in tomorrow for tomorrow is yet to come. Today is all you have; it is within your power to take hold of the opportunities it brings to be the best you can and to refuse to be defeated.

Like Sylvia, it is possible that at some time or other your life has been brought low by circumstances beyond your control. At the same time, you may have been touched by the love of God that passed by unrecognized because it appeared in an unexpected way. Sometimes that love touches us through people or extraordinary circumstances, as it did in Sylvia's case.

Finally, remember that miracles do happen. Be encouraged in the knowledge that you are of infinite value and your life is worth living. Be inspired by the declaration made by Sir Winston Churchill towards the end of the Second World War in the time of Britain's darkest hour: 'Success is not final. Failure is not fatal. It is the courage to continue that counts.'

It is possible that if you forgive and are forgiven, you will

find your own MISSING PEACE.

Lightning Source UK Ltd.
Milton Keynes UK
UKHW022216300520
364099UK00003B/362